1976 £20

GW01451552

1976 £20

The Embroidery
of Mexico
and Guatemala

The Embroidery of Mexico and Guatemala

Frances Schaill Goodman

Charles Scribner's Sons   New York

Copyright © 1976 Frances Schaill Goodman

Library of Congress Cataloging in Publication Data

Goodman, Frances Schaill.
    The embroidery of Mexico and Guatemala.

    Includes index.
    1. Indians of Mexico—Textile industry and fab-
rics. 2. Indians of Central America—Guatemala—
Textile industry and fabrics. 3. Embroidery—Mexico.
4. Embroidery—Central America. I. Title.
F1219.3.T4G66   746.4′4′0972   75-29325
ISBN 0-684-14498-0

This book published simultaneously in the
United States of America and in Canada—
Copyright under the Berne Convention

All rights reserved. No part of this book
may be reproduced in any form without the
permission of Charles Scribner's Sons.

1 3 5 7 9 11 13 15 17 19 MD / C 20 18 16 14 12 10 8 6 4 2

Printed in the United States of America

To all the women of
Mexico and Guatemala
whose deft fingers
have created so much beauty

﷽ Contents ﷽

ACKNOWLEDGMENTS

Many, many people helped me in many ways with this project. I wish especially to thank:

Anne Seelbach and other members of the staff of the Costume Institute of the Metropolitan Museum of Art who were helpful in locating material and advising me.

Claudia Medoff and her staff of the University of Pennsylvania Museum for all the time and trouble they took to help me.

The Brooklyn Museum Library and Mrs. Peggy Zorach.

Tonatiuh Gutiérrez and members of his staff at the Fondo Nacional para el Fomento Artesanal, in Mexico City, who offered every courtesy in my quest.

Ruth Erickson, who opened her collection to my inspection.

The Textile Museum in Washington, D.C.

The Mexican National Tourist Council, for photographs.

Mexico's Museo Nacional de Antropologia for its permission to photograph its exhibits.

Dea Mungia de Greaves and Ruth Sample de Gutiérrez for their T.L.C., advice, chauffeuring, and many other kindnesses.

Dell Feuerlicht for his generous loan of photographs from his collection.

Harold Johnson for his drawings.

Charles Dorkins for his patience and his beautiful photographs.

Roland Goodman for aid and comfort and help far beyond any call of duty.

The Embroidery
of Mexico
and Guatemala

A Heritage of Craft

From one end of Mexico and Guatemala to the other, busy needles are turning out quantities of embroidery. In the sophisticated cities, the aprons, tablecloths, and petit-point cushions can hardly be distinguished from those being made in the United States and western Europe, for even embroidery patterns know no national boundaries in our modern world.

In these two countries, however, older ways still survive among the rural people. This book focuses on the products of that fast-disappearing life-style. Removed in time if not in space, it is embroidery that grows out of tradition. I am happy to have the opportunity to record through photographs a sampling of an art that is changing and dying year by year.

The rich and varied traditional embroidery of Mexico and Guatemala is a folk art, and that's an important fact to remember. Skills with the needle are passed down from mother to daughter—and, in a few instances, from father to son. The designs often have a symbolic meaning, and may have originated centuries ago. There have been changes and new ideas, but these have been instigated largely by outside influences.

Besides being traditional, folk art expresses itself in articles that are part of the life of the people who produce it. A pottery jug can do its basic job of holding water even if it is

1

ugly and misshapen. But the people who make their own water jugs, anywhere on earth, seem to be instinctively impelled to make them graceful, and often to add attractive decorations as well.

So it is with traditional Mexican and Guatemalan embroidery. It is applied to clothing and other household fabrics, which in many communities are still woven by hand, sometimes from homespun thread. The stitchery itself, colorful and interesting, makes light weight of its burden of history.

To understand and appreciate this embroidery, then, you must know something of the roots from which it grows. In subsequent chapters I shall tell about the weaving and costumes before passing on to the designs themselves. But first let us take a look at the countries and the people.

Mexico, our southern neighbor, is large, with more than one-fifth the area and population of the United States. Guatemala, about the size of Ohio, has four and a half million people; it lies just south of Mexico, which it has been known to call "the colossus of the north." What they have in common is central mountains and rain-forested lowlands that separated the original Indian population into more or less isolated groups speaking at least threescore languages. This subdivision could go even further—the Mam-speaking Indians of the western Guatemalan highlands, who are cousins of the Mayans, live in twenty-three communities separated by mountain ridges, and each village has its own distinctive costumes!

In fact, life-styles did not differ as much as did costumes. Allowing for variations in climate, the Indians had similar crops, houses, and religions. The diversity came chiefly in matters like folk art and clothing.

Some six centuries ago the area had two major nations—the Aztecs in central Mexico and the Mayans in southern Mexico and parts of Guatemala—as well as many lesser ones. It would be a mistake to call their civilization primitive, although it developed differently from that of Europe.

They had no beasts of burden, had never developed the wheel, and were without metal tools (except a few copper implements). But their mathematicians had worked out the concept of zero while Europe was still struggling with clumsy Roman numerals. Their astronomers accurately predicted eclipses of the sun and moon and charted the path of Venus. Their architects erected stupendous temples. And sophisticated political systems kept the major nations functioning.

Above all, these people were artists. Gold, silver, and semiprecious stones were made into delicate jewelry. Sculptors carved stone and wood both sensitively and monumentally.

Powerful paintings and shapely stucco figures decorated the temples. Potters and leather workers plied their trades. And, pertinent to the subject of this book, these Indians were adept at spinning, weaving, and fashioning elaborate garments.

In 1519, a Spaniard named Hernando Cortés landed at what is now Veracruz, on the Gulf of Mexico, with a few hundred soldiers. Shrewd and possessed of gunpowder, horses, and superior military skill, Cortés within a few years had conquered much of Mexico and Central America. The kings of Spain ruled these lands for three centuries until they gained their independence in 1821.

The Spaniards valued the Indians' handicrafts, for their own use and for the profits to be made in exporting them. And the conquerors of course brought along their own arts, materials, and techniques. The two cultures persisted side by side, despite much mingling, and even today the differences have survived, as we shall see in the weaving and embroidery.

But the conditions of the conquest—it is said that in three centuries there were never more than fifty thousand Spaniards in Mexico at any one time—created something totally new. That something is the mestizo, the person of mixed European and Indian descent. The mestizo, energetic and inventive, has made the modern and industrialized Mexico

of today. But he also lives in the quieter countryside and small towns, where his artistic sensitivity manifests itself in a culture that is neither Spanish nor Indian.

In deeper isolation, most often in the mountains and roadless coastal slopes, many Indian communities survive, holding to their ancient languages and traditions. But Mexico is steadily extending its highway network. Buses with modest fares carry the villager in an hour to the market town that once was a hard day's walk away, while the outside world invades the settlement's privacy and nibbles away at the old customs.

There has been a happy new development in recent years, however. Modern Mexico has reawakened to the worth of its manifold heritage. The government is dedicated to carrying such benefits as education and health care to the most remote corners of the country, but it is doing so with an awareness that traditional ways of life have values that deserve to be preserved. In particular, the government takes a lively and intelligent interest in handicrafts. It doesn't merely preserve the finest examples in museums. It encourages their production, acts to revive those that are in danger of dying out, monitors their quality to make sure that designs and techniques do not degenerate. Eminently practical, government agencies help to market the output, enhancing the income of the craftsmen while providing exports to aid the national economy.

Guatemala is different. Poorer and smaller than Mexico, it is less far along in its industrial development. Half the population are Indians, whose traditions and crafts have survived with a minimum of dilution.

Coming back to my opening theme, the embroidery of these countries has meaning chiefly against the cultural backgrounds and in relation to the traditional textiles and costumes. Thus I shall trace these underlying elements before going on to a detailed description of the needlework.

Plate 1. A Guatemalan
woman weaving on a hip loom.
(Photograph: Dell Feuerlicht)

Plate 2. The marketplace is a
social center, and a Guatemalan
woman puts on her best everyday *huipil*
to go shopping. (Photograph:
Dell Feuerlicht)

Plate 3 (*left*). A group of men from Chichicastenango, Guatemala, in full ceremonial costume. (Photograph: R. Mata, courtesy of "La Helvetia")

Plate 4 (*below*). A Guatemalan woman stitches a *randa* outside her home. Faintly visible in the background is a hip loom. (Photograph: Dell Feuerlicht)

Plate 5. Eagle on Huichol man's shirt. (Courtesy, Fondo Nacional para el Fomento Artesanal, Mexico City; photograph: Charles Dorkins)

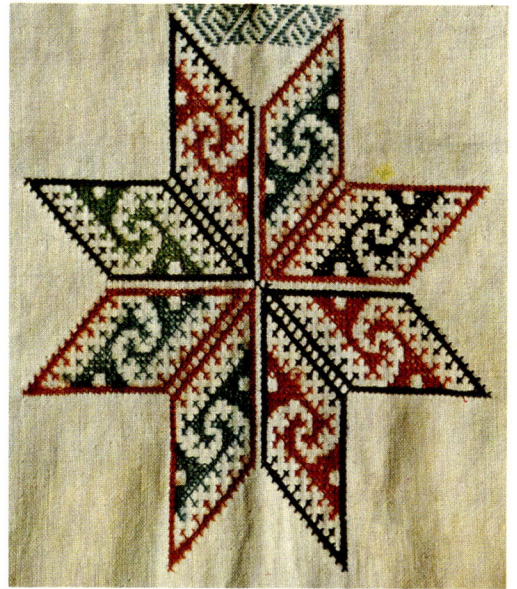

Plate 8. Cross on Huichol woman's *huipil*. (Courtesy, Metropolitan Museum of Art, New York; photograph: Charles Dorkins)

Plate 6. Peacocks on Huichol man's shawl. (Courtesy, Fondo Nacional para el Fomento Artesanal, Mexico City; photograph: Charles Dorkins)

Plate 7. Female figure on Huichol woman's *huipil*. (Courtesy, Metropolitan Museum of Art, New York; photograph: Charles Dorkins)

Plate 9 (*above*).   A frequently recurring design in traditional work from the Sierra de Puebla region in central Mexico is this *flor de piña*, here surrounded by other designs. (Collection of the author; photograph: Charles Dorkins)

Plate 10 (*right*).   The "tree of life," usually growing from a flowerpot, is another traditional theme from the Sierra de Puebla. This and the previous example are Otomi Indian embroidery. (Collection of the author; photograph: Charles Dorkins)

8

Plates 11 and 12. The front (above) and back (right) of this table cover demonstrate the evenness of the work. From the Mazahua area of Mexico's Sierra de Puebla, it includes the ancient double cross as well as birds and mammals. (Courtesy, Fondo Nacional para el Fomento Artesanal, Mexico City; photographs: Charles Dorkins)

9

Plate 13.   Satin stitch predominates in this *huipil* from Santa María Sacatepequez, Guatemala.
(Ruth Erickson collection; photograph: Charles Dorkins)

10

Plate 14. *Muñeca*, or doll, is what these tiny figures, no more than an inch and a quarter high, are called in Spanish. These are from the short pants worn by the men of Santiago Atitlán, Guatemala. (Courtesy, Metropolitan Museum of Art, New York; photograph: Charles Dorkins)

Plate 15. Row on row of tiny birds decorate the front of a man's pants from Zacatepec, Mexico. (Ruth Erickson collection; photograph: Charles Dorkins)

Plate 16. *Hazme si puedes*—"make me if you can"—is the appropriate name for the intricate smocking on this blouse from Ocotlán in Mexico's state of Oaxaca. (Courtesy, Fondo Nacional para el Fomento Artesanal, Mexico City; photograph: Charles Dorkins)

Plate 17. A striking example of couching on a colorful *quech-quemitl* from Tancanhuitz, Mexico. (Courtesy, Museo Nacional de Antropologia, Mexico City; photograph: Charles Dorkins)

Plate 18.   The figures on this *tzut* from Chichicastenango, Guatemala, are fertility symbols, indicating that it was used in formal ceremonies. (Courtesy, University of Pennsylvania Museum; photograph: Charles Dorkins)

Plate 19.   Front and back views of segments of two six-foot-long belts from Nahualá, Guatemala, embroidered in heavy wool. (Courtesy, Metropolitan Museum of Art, New York; photograph: Charles Dorkins)

13

Plate 20 (*above*). Done by the men of
Chichicastenango, Guatemala, this is perhaps
the most superb embroidery of the region
covered by this book. (Courtesy, Metropolitan
Museum of Art, New York; photograph:
Charles Dorkins)

Plate 21 (below). The closeup of this peacock
from Ojitlán, Oaxaca, shows clearly the open
weave of the cloth and the striking yet simple
embroidery. (Courtesy, Fondo Nacional para el
Fomento Artesanal, Mexico City; photograph:
Charles Dorkins)

Plate 22 (*right*). An embroidered zigzag fills
out the woven pattern of this *huipil* from a
Mexican village with the tongue-twisting name of
Xochistlahuaca. (Courtesy, Fondo Nacional para
el Fomento Artesanal, Mexico City; photograph:
Charles Dorkins)

Plate 23. Detail of a large *huipil*, made of a gauzelike fabric, from Quezaltenango, Guatemala. (Courtesy, University of Pennsylvania Museum; photograph: Charles Dorkins)

Plate 24. This *randa* from Zunil, Guatemala, is done unusually in two different widths. (Courtesy, University of Pennsylvania Museum; photograph: Charles Dorkins)

Plate 25. The *randas* run both horizontally and vertically on a skirt from Venustiano Carranza, in southern Mexico. (Courtesy, Fondo Nacional para el Fomento Artesanal, Mexico City; photograph: Charles Dorkins)

Plate 26. Symbolism overflows on this classic *huipil* from Chichicastenango, Guatemala—sun, moons, corn plants, double crosses, a two-headed bird, a lightning zigzag. (Courtesy, University of Pennsylvania Museum; photograph: Charles Dorkins)

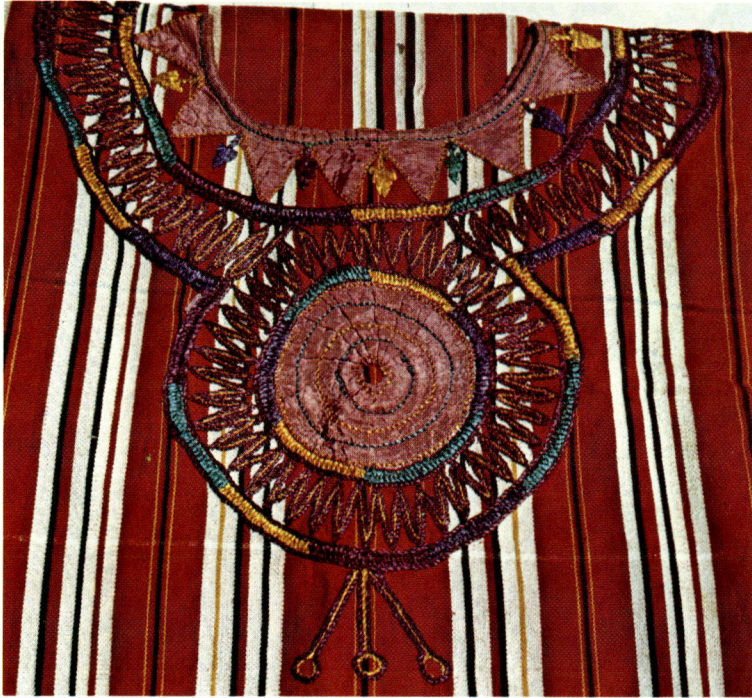

Plate 27.   This complex design decorates the front of a *huipil* from Sololá, Guatemala. (Courtesy, University of Pennsylvania Museum; photograph: Charles Dorkins)

Plate 28.   An overwhelming amount of hand-done chain stitch covers a *huipil* from Tehuantepec, Mexico, of which only a portion is shown in this photograph. (Ruth Erickson collection; photograph: Charles Dorkins)

Plate 29. The colorful embroidery on this *huipil* from Zumpango, Mexico, is done in buttonhole, chain, and satin stitches. (Courtesy, University of Pennsylvania Museum; photograph: Charles Dorkins)

Plate 30. The natural brown cotton of this hand-woven *huipil* from Chichicas-tenango, Guatemala, is native to the Americas, but is rarely seen nowadays. (Courtesy, University of Pennsylvania Museum; photograph: Charles Dorkins)

Plate 31. No less than eleven concentric circles of embroidery surround the neckline of this *huipil* from Joyabaj, Guatemala. (Courtesy, University of Pennsylvania Museum; photograph: Charles Dorkins)

Plate 32. This sunlike motif is traditional and is embroidered by the men of Chichicastenango, Guatemala, on the flap that stands out at the side of their short pants. (Courtesy, Metropolitan Museum of Art, New York; photograph: Charles Dorkins)

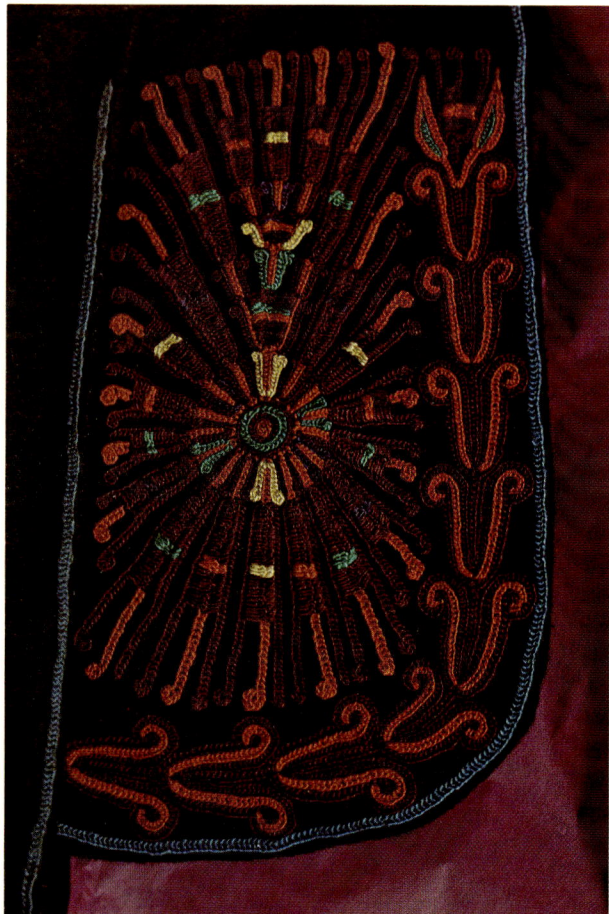

Plate 33. This example of needle weaving, or drawn work, appears in a piece of edging made to be attached to the long *huipil* of Yucatán in Mexico. (Courtesy, Fondo Nacional para el Fomento Artesanal, Mexico City; photograph: Charles Dorkins)

Plate 34. The front of a man's shirt from Zacatepec, Mexico, offers another example of needle weaving. (Ruth Erickson collection; photograph: Charles Dorkins)

The Classic Textiles

An eyewitness account of pre-Spanish crafts was provided by Bernal Díaz del Castillo, a doughty soldier who served under Cortés from the beginning and sat down in his old age to chronicle the campaigns. Díaz tells of the many conciliatory gifts that Montezuma, the Aztec emperor, sent to Cortés, including "ten pack loads of white cotton cloth, decorated with feathers that were wonderful to see" and "twenty loads of fine cotton cloth."

In describing the Aztecs' crafts, Díaz speaks of "Indian women, weavers or seamstresses, who made such a multitude of fine clothing with great amounts of featherwork, most of which came almost daily from some towns and the province on the north coast," near Veracruz.

"In the great Montezuma's own house all the daughters of chiefs whom he had as mistresses always wove excellent things," Díaz adds. "Many daughters of neighboring Mexicans who were there in a sort of seclusion, something like nuns, also did weaving, all with feathers."

The Aztec soldiers, he says, had armor of quilted cotton. On the other hand, the people of the little independent mountain nation of Tlaxcala, impoverished by its struggles to fend off the Aztecs, wove their cloth of henequen, a coarse fiber, "because they did not have cotton." Díaz also mentions a map painted on henequen cloth.

In this busy Guatemalan market, the seated woman vendor is wearing an embroidered blouse. (Photograph: Dell Feuerlicht)

But Díaz says nothing of embroidery. In the featherwork that impressed him so much —some examples survive from the conquest period—the shafts of the feathers are worked into the cloth, with the plumes hanging down in overlapping rows. Today, in Chiapas, the only Mexican state where there is a surviving tradition of making feathered cloth, the entire feathers are woven into the fabric, forming a border.

The other principal sources of information about pre-Spanish textiles in Mexico and Guatemala are the surviving codices, sculpture, wall paintings, and pottery, plus the accounts of a few Spanish priests who wrote some time after the conquest. A codex is the nearest thing to a book that was produced by the more advanced peoples of Middle America. It was made of either deerskin parchment or a crude cactus-fiber paper and was often folded accordion-style into pages. These early peoples had not developed alphabets, but used hieroglyphs or picture writing. A few codices have been preserved in museums. At least one of them lists the tribute that various towns paid to the Aztec emperor, including such items as four hundred blankets annually, confirming that weaving was a thriving activity.

Similarly, the sculptures, painting, and pottery depict people wearing garments made of textiles or animal skins, but they do not enable us to decipher details. It is obvious, however, that narrow pieces of cloth were sewn together with the thorn, bone, or copper needles that were used in pre-Spanish days.

While it may seem logical that people who had needles would use them to embroider designs, the only embroidery that can be identified from those times is the *randa*, a stitch used to fasten two edges together without overlapping, especially in skirts. One priestly account tells of embroidered sandals, however.

Extremely little weaving from early Middle America has survived. Various feather capes are in modern museums, and archaeologists have found a few bits and pieces of more utilitarian cloth. In the relatively damp climate, fibers, wood, leather, and fur rotted away over the centuries. This is in contrast to Peru, where ancient graves in the bone-dry coastal desert have yielded up quantities of handsome and technically complex weaving and embroidery.

But there is ample evidence of spinning and weaving activity in ancient Mexican and

Guatemalan relics, if not of the textiles themselves. The potters and sculptors often showed people at everyday activities. These include women at their looms, wearing garments and headdresses that are often similar to those in use today. The equipment—spinning whorls, looms, and combs for the warp—is readily recognizable. And baked clay whorls are often found in ancient sites.

Besides the cotton and henequen mentioned by Díaz, ixtle was another native fiber. The long, fleshy leaves of the maguey—the familiar century plant—were shredded to extract the ixtle. Henequen is a plant about three feet tall, similar to the Asian plants that are the source of jute. The stems are soaked and shredded to separate the fiber, which is now used mostly to make rope.

Cotton is one of the few plants indigenous to both the Eastern and Western Hemispheres. Middle America has not only the familiar white cotton, but also a golden brown variety which is still cultivated in limited amounts. Cotton remains one of Mexico's most important crops today.

Besides the brilliantly colored feathers of tropical birds, the ancient Mexicans also wove rabbit fur and strips of leather into their cloth. These were both decorative and warm.

Spinning by hand has not changed since ancient times. A slim pointed stick, weighted with a small clay whorl, is used. The point may be rested in a half-gourd, or the stick may dangle free if a woman is spinning as she walks to market or watches over a flock. The Spanish introduced some spinning wheels of the sort that collectors of early Americana thirst after, but they are rare, and I believe they are used mostly to spin wool.

Before the Spaniards came, and for many years thereafter, the Middle American Indians employed a wide variety of natural dyes. Some of these are still used today. Indigo, which in concentrated form makes navy blue and, when diluted, lighter blues, is extracted from the leaves and stems of several different native bushes. Fruits and roots, wood and bark, from many varieties of trees and smaller plants provide all the other colors except green, which is a mixture of indigo blue and one of several available yellows.

Only two animals, cochineal and murex, are sources of dyes. Cochineal is a scale insect that lives on the nopal cactus (the one with flat oval leaves that is a symbol of Mexico). Cochineal farming was once a major activity, with fields of nopal covered with "herds" that grew from egg to adult in about three months in the dry season, four in the rainy season. The adults were scraped off the leaves, killed by heat, dried, and sold by the ounce. They could then be soaked in water to extract the bright red dye.

Cochineal was a major export of Middle America from the seventeenth to the late nineteenth centuries. At one time Queen Elizabeth I forbade further imports of it to England because so much was already on hand. John Lloyd Stephens, an American who wrote an engaging book about his travels in Central America in 1839–40, told of the cochineal plantations in Guatemala. This industry has virtually vanished today, although I have found the insects growing wild on nopals near Oaxaca, Mexico. The invention and wide marketing of aniline dyes toward the end of the nineteenth century sharply curtailed the demand, and by the beginning

Mayan goddess of weaving, with hip loom (from Codex Tro-Cortesianus).

of this century these chemical dyes had invaded Central America, greatly reducing the use of the natural colorings that were often laborious to collect and prepare.

The other animal dye is obtained from the murex, a snail-like mollusk with a number of species that inhabit the tropical seas around the world. This is where the Romans got their Tyrian purple of imperial renown. It was a shortage of these shellfish that drove the Phoenicians to seek farther and farther along the shores of the Mediterranean and incidentally discover the full boundaries of that sea. A gland in the murex exudes a few drops of a fast purple dye, and after a rest it will give up a few more drops. Some few can still be found on the rocks along the Pacific shore of the Mexican state of Oaxaca. The Huave Indians of that area take skeins of thread to the shore, coax the murex to deposit its dye directly onto the thread, and put the animals back on the rocks to await another milking.

Weaving in preconquest times was generally done on the hip loom (it has many other names), which is still widely used today. It is an ingenious, simple, and yet very effective loom that is easily portable. The hip loom's chief drawback is that it rarely makes cloth wider than twenty-four inches, the greatest distance that the weaver can conveniently reach from side to side, or longer than seven or eight feet, the most that can be handily rolled up as it is completed. Traditionally, women have been the weavers, but men occasionally take part. See colorplate 1.

The weaver ties the warp threads, neatly spaced, to a stick at each end, passing them through the heddle's loops. At the far end, ropes are attached, and these are tied around a post or tree. A belt is fastened to the near end, and this goes around the hips of the weaver, whose body maintains the tension on the warp. The woven cloth is wound around the stick in front of the weaver as it is finished.

The heddle, through which the warp threads pass so that their positions can be shifted as the weft is inserted, has loops of string tied to a slender stick. One or more shuttles for feeding in the weft threads, plus a couple of wide, smooth battens to push the weft snugly into place, complete the basic parts of the hip loom. This is the simple equipment that the rural folk of Mexico and Guate-

An example of Guatemalan finger weaving. (Collection of the author; photograph: Charles Dorkins)

mala have used over the centuries to produce cloth that is often intricately woven.

Not only can hip-loomed textiles range from very coarse to very fine, but many varieties of openwork, including gauze, can be made by twisting the warp in certain ways. Adjustments of the warp can also achieve diaper patterns, surface stripes, damask, brocade, tapestry, and other effects.

Returning to the fabric itself, there is one special sort of work that is of particular interest to us. This is known as finger weaving or loom embroidery.

The weaver has separate hanks of colored threads and inserts them by hand across a limited number of warp threads to make a design. After each single-thread insertion the weft shuttle is thrown across, and the weft and inserted threads are battened down.

The completed figures look very much like needle embroidery, but there are ways to tell them apart. For one, the finger-woven threads are always parallel to the weft and are separated by weft threads. For another, any attempt to create exactly the same effect with a needle is likely to cross the threads unevenly here and there, and may even fail to be fitted in between every pair of weft threads. The accuracy and deftness of the experienced hip-loom operator may well carry over to her embroidery, however, so a close inspection may be necessary.

Indian Costume, Past and Present

One of the great fascinations of Mexico and Guatemala is the survival of ancient ways of life alongside a sophisticated and modern civilization. The most striking survival is the wide array of colorful costumes. These have certainly been affected by outside influences, but they retain many of their original features.

One change was the introduction of new textile fibers. Cortés brought in silkworms, but this effort faded out, and Spain later forbade silk culture in the colonies. On the other hand, sheep were an important contribution. They throve, and soon wool was plentiful. It was a welcome innovation, because the weather can be quite cold in the highlands of Mexico and Guatemala.

The Spanish also had a strong impact on the manufacture of textiles. They continued and expanded the Aztec system of exacting tribute in the form of goods from the communities under their rule, including quantities of fabrics. (Just one area, Choapán in the state of Oaxaca, was said to have been forced to supply sixteen thousand lengths of fabric every two months.) The conquerors introduced the framed standing loom for producing wide textiles and must have provided new designs, as well as ordered alterations in traditional patterns to suit their own preferences. Even today, in isolated areas where the women still weave as their ancestors did, textile motifs range from purely Indian to totally Spanish in their inspiration.

Guatemalan man weaving on
a standing loom.
(Photograph: Dell Feuerlicht)

In the Indian garments themselves, men's clothing has changed the most. Before the conquest, it consisted basically of a loincloth and a rectangular cloth that wrapped around under one arm and was knotted on the opposite shoulder to form a cape called a *tilmatl*, which the Spanish shortened to *tilma*. Both loincloth and *tilma* are rare today (a few men have a *tilma*-like garment called an *ayate*, made of ixtle fiber).

Nearly all Indian men now wear some sort of trousers and shirts, which are often strikingly distinctive and colorful in their design and decoration. For the women, the *huipil*, skirt, and *quechquemitl* survive from pre-Spanish times, as do belts and various hair arrangements.

Indian clothes are based on the rectangle, and the fabric is clasically narrow if it is still woven on the hip loom. Today, however, some fabrics are woven on the wider-framed standing loom, and the women may even buy factory-made cloth.

The *huipil*, the woman's blouse, is essentially a rectangle that is doubled and sewn up the sides, leaving an opening for the arms. If it is made of a single width of cloth, a slit or round hole is cut for the neck. If made of

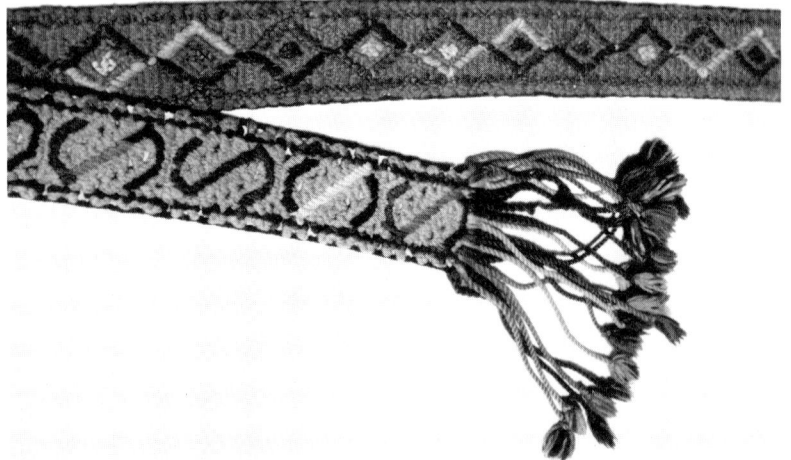

A hand-woven Mexican belt.
(Courtesy, University of Pennsylvania Museum; photograph: Charles Dorkins)

26

two pieces of cloth, the seam runs vertically down the center and is interrupted to leave a slit for the neck; for three widths, the opening may be a slit or round hole. The *huipil* can be short, barely waist length (see color-plate 2), or it may hang to the ankles and be worn without a skirt.

The skirt—*falda* or *refajo*—is a long piece of cloth with the ends connected. The woman steps inside it and wraps it around her body. If it is very long, she will pleat or fold it to fit at the waist; if short, it may be fastened like a sarong. A long, handsome woven belt is used to hold the skirt up. The *huipil* sometimes is tucked under the skirt and sometimes hangs over it. Since hip-loom fabric is narrow and is used horizontally in a skirt, two pieces are normally sewn together selvedge to selvedge with a decorative *randa* in order to make the skirt long enough. A great many traditional skirts are navy blue broken only by a few pinstripes, so the *randa*—perhaps two or two and a half inches of brighter colors—makes a happy accent. See color-plate 4.

The *quechquemitl* is known nowhere in the world except Middle America, almost entirely in Mexico. It is virtually nonexistent in Guatemala and in Mexico's Yucatán; both of these areas have a Mayan heritage, so the reason is probably a difference in cultural background.

The *quechquemitl* is an upper garment that gives the effect of a cape, with triangles over the chest and back. It may vary in size and can be worn with or without a *huipil*. Sometimes, too, it is folded on top of the head to keep off the sun, or for ceremonial purposes.

In fact, the *quechquemitl* is a very cleverly made garment. Most often it consists of two rectangles. The short side of one piece is attached to the end of the long side of the other piece. Then the free end of the second piece is brought around to be attached to the near long side of the first piece. The result is a rounded cone with an opening for the head, and two points that hang down in front and back. It is a warm, comfortable garment that stays in place.

There are several variations on the basic construction, of which the most remarkable is found in some villages where the weaving is made to go around a corner! The *quechquemitl* can be woven decoratively, but because of its shape it is the garment most often embellished with embroidery.

The ubiquitous rebozo of Mexican fame, a long, ample scarf, is a concept imported from Spain. I know of only one place, Hueyapán and environs in the state of Puebla, where the rebozo, of hand-spun black wool and embroidered in cross-stitch, has become a part of the indigenous costume.

Men's garments, besides shirts and short or long trousers, sometimes include jackets or ponchos. Even in villages where the women's garments are always made from home-woven fabrics, the manufacture of men's shirts and trousers may vary greatly. At one extreme, the cloth may be hand-woven from thread that is spun and dyed in

Mexican woman in *quechquemitl*.

the village. Or the thread may be bought for looming at home. These fabrics often have colorful patterns. At the other extreme, the garments may be made at home from commercially produced *manta*—unbleached muslin—or the garments may be bought ready-made. In any case, the cut of the shirts and trousers is likely to be simplified, so that the fit is indifferent.

Manta shirts are often decorated with machine-sewn embroidery. This is no more than ordinary machine stitching in color, gone over several times to make a heavier line, creating a pattern or a border. The hand-woven fabrics, on the other hand, may be done in stripes, such as red and white, or even in a widely spaced plaid with finger embroidery in the squares. Some few are hand-embroidered.

Jackets are highly decorative in some Guatemalan villages, being made of hand-woven dark wool or red commercial cotton cloth with black braid embellishments.

Men from the chilly highlands sometimes also wear a very narrow wraparound apron of heavy hand-loomed wool over their trousers. In combination with a jacket, this makes an impressive and warm outfit.

The serape—essentially a moderate-size blanket—is a woven rectangle of wool, and thus is a postconquest introduction. With a center slit so that it can be put on over the head like a poncho, it formerly was a common men's garment in colder areas. Each geographical area had its characteristic colors and patterns for serapes. Thus, although there were many minor variations, it was possible to say that a particular serape came from a specific region. The dilution of traditional styles makes such identification much less feasible today.

The *capexii*, another outer garment for men, worn in southern Mexico and Guatemala, has elements of both the jacket and serape. It is a rectangle of heavy felted wool doubled over with a slit for the head, with two sleeves sewn on. The sides are stitched together up to the armpit, which is left open to allow freedom of motion. It is a warm

Man from Sololá, Guatemala, with apron over trousers.

garment, comfortable for sleeping as well as for working in the chill of early morning or late afternoon.

The costume of the men of Chichicastenango, in the mountains of Guatemala, deserves special mention. There is nothing else just like it, now or in the past, although I understand that there was a vaguely similar Spanish peasant costume of the sixteenth century that could have been remembered by an unknown priest or colonist who might have helped to devise the Chichicastenango outfit. See colorplate 3.

The basic garments are a simply cut cotton shirt, white or striped, and a pair of knee-length pants of heavy black wool cut rather intricately, with an expansive seat but tapered to the knee. Set into the outside seams of the pants are flanges that jut out sideways and are embroidered. In the front is a yoke that fastens around the waist with buttons.

The Chichicastenango man's jacket is made of the same wool as the pants and reaches just below the waist. Its back panel ends in a short fringe. The sleeves are long, with embroidery on the sides of the jacket, the shoulder seams, and the chest. A head covering called a *tzut*, wrapped around like a turban, tops off a costume that is magnificently impressive on these short but sturdily built people.

These garments are made and embroidered by the Chichicastenango men themselves. The embroidery is mostly in orange, red, and purple silk or rayon, in a small, even, and neat chain stitch. The designs are traditional —a sun on the chest and flowers on the sides.

Finally, there is the *servilleta*—literally, napkin. Basically it is an all-purpose square of cloth for carrying things. Anywhere from twelve by twelve to forty by forty inches, it is indispensable in a culture where paper is scarce. Traditionally, there were separate *servilletas* for different purposes, and each had a special name related to its use. For example, *tzut* is the name for the cloth that the Chichicastenango men wear on their heads for ceremonial purposes. Some others were for special occasions, such as carrying candles to church or transporting seed corn. Others were used to wrap tortillas, or as a sling to carry a baby on a mother's back, or as coverings for head or shoulders. Many *servilletas* are embroidered decoratively, most often with traditional designs. Both men and women use them.

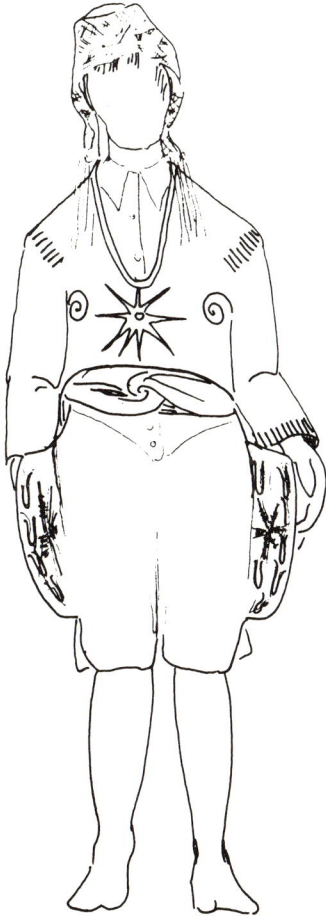

Man from Chichicastenango, Guatemala.

Tradition and Individuality

The steep mountain ranges that divide the populated valleys and plateaus of Mexico and Guatemala made travel and communication difficult until well into this century. Only the major population centers and ports were linked by railroads, or by roads suitable for wheeled vehicles. Foot and horse trails connected the smaller communities.

The Spanish and their Europeanized mestizo descendants preempted the best and most accessible land. The Indians who were able to preserve their customs and ancient way of life relatively unchanged were those in remote areas, mostly in the highlands. The Spanish kept an eye on them, and the Indians became converts to Catholicism, which is now practiced universally, even where remnants of the old beliefs and rituals survive. But the people, poor and with few beasts of burden, were largely isolated. Some still are, although they enjoy making treks on foot to fiestas and to market towns where they can sell their products and buy a few necessities.

It is this isolation that we can thank for the survival of costumes with little change over the centuries. Of course this includes the embroidery; by far the richest source of distinctive designs in these countries is the Indian villages.

The original reason that each preconquest village had its own costumes is unclear; perhaps in order to tell friend from foe in battle, or perhaps the tendency toward uniformity in an isolated and tradition-oriented community. Again it is only conjecture, but the Spanish may have encouraged the custom—once they had converted the men to respectable Christian trousers—so that they could be aware of unusual movements among the people (danger!). Or these explanations may be unnecessarily complex; it may have been just a combination of local pride and availability of materials. We can get no clue from the instances of women who marry into another village. Sometimes they retain their original costumes; sometimes they adopt those of their new homes.

It is still possible in Guatemala to tell which villages most Indians come from by a glance at their clothes. That is also true for many communities in Mexico, but the number is dwindling. An example is the Chamula women in Chiapas, with their heavy woolen skirts and *huipils*, most often blackish brown, and with folded wool cloths balanced on their heads. They seem to personify the cold and glowering climate of their home plateau, and they contrast strongly with their neighbors whose homes are more sheltered.

Chamula woman in embroidered woolen *huipil*. (Photograph: Dell Feuerlicht)

Extensive road-building and cheap bus transportation have brought many once-isolated Mexicans into the mainstream of national life. The spread of political freedom and social mobility has broken down regional barriers and customs. Nevertheless, Mexico remains a country that respects individuality. People may wear what they please without censure, and some places that are well aware of the modern world have chosen to cling to their traditional garments. Others reserve them chiefly for fiesta or holiday wear. The government's efforts to preserve craftsmanship also help to keep alive the villagers' skill at embroidery.

As mentioned in the first chapter, Guatemala is another story. It has less money to build roads, so many areas are still shut away. Nevertheless, although 50 per cent of the population is pure Indian and still speaks the Indian languages, the areas along the tourist routes are losing their standards of both workmanship and symbolism in favor of speed and financial return. So the individuality of most of the Guatemalan costumes is fading fast.

Many of the symbols in Guatemalan and Mexican weaving and embroidery date back before the Spanish conquest, and many of the people recognize them as such. They are not copied out of habit, but in an awareness of their meaning.

The lightning symbol, signifying fertility, appears often in both weaving and embroidery. But the Indians are not inclined to discuss such matters with strangers. One day in Guatemala I encountered a woman with a prominent lightning design on her *huipil*. I was in an earnest scholarly mood that day, so I decided to draw her into a discussion of it, while enlarging my vocabulary of Indian words.

"What do you call that design?" I asked in Spanish.

"Well," she said, "I don't know what you might call it, but we call it zigzag."

Somehow, my scholarship died a-borning.

An *S* lying on its side is also symbolic, standing for a worm or perhaps a snake. In any event, it is a bringer of good tidings. (A similar form, its meaning unclear, is found in early Greek decoration.)

Many round *huipil* necklines are finished with a circle of points, sometimes appliquéd and sometimes embroidered. These represent the sun and are much like the pattern found on the famous Aztec calendar stone (see photo on page 69) and other preconquest sculpture.

Also, *huipils* occasionally have ribbon ap-

Lightning, snake, and cross symbols adorn this *quechquemitl* from central Mexico. (Courtesy, Museo Nacional de Antropologia, Mexico City; photograph: Charles Dorkins)

pliquéd circles—and at times half-circles—on the shoulders and front. These stand for the moon and its phases. For some reason this symbol is rarely embroidered.

The double-headed bird needs to be mentioned. At first glance it seems very Spanish, since the two-headed eagle dominates the coat-of-arms of the Hapsburg kings of Spain. But to some Indians it is an ancient symbol that is linked to their animistic beliefs. Whatever the reason for its use, it is a most effective motif artistically (see photo on page 42).

The cross also has a preconquest as well as a Christian derivation. In the ancestral sense it represents the cardinal points of the compass and has two horizontals and two verticals—in effect, a double cross. Or it may be the four sides of the *milpa*, the corn patch that is the heart of Indian agriculture. The embroidered area of many a *huipil* forms a cross (see colorplate 26). The cross appears comparatively rarely in the Christian form of two simple bars. Most often it is decorated with flowers or leaves, which in some instances may be an inheritance of the foliated crosses that are carved on Mayan stone monuments (see photo on page 41).

This only touches on the broad range of symbolism in Guatemala's and Mexico's Indian textiles and embroidery.

Two odd facts about Guatemalan costume: Many villages with distinctive garb have given up weaving, instead buying their textiles from weaving centers that make the fabrics—especially skirt and belt lengths—to suit specific needs. At the other extreme, many weavers who are proud of their craftsmanship sign their textiles with tiny finger-embroidered figures, usually at the bottom.

It is to be hoped that crafts have not been disrupted by the tragic earthquakes of early 1976, which severely damaged many mountain communities, including Chichicastenango.

The Blending
of Lifestreams

Tradition is an integral part of folk art. Tradition might be defined as using the available materials to their fullest and, through experience, to their best. Tradition in design is based on a combination of use, cult and inheritance, custom, and craft.

Tradition can absorb some new materials and some new cultural ideas, but when the mixture gets too thin most of the cultural value is lost or changed. There is always a point, if this happens, where the folk art ceases to be of traditional artistic value. It then becomes characterless—or something worthwhile but different that has a place of its own.

The craft element is the workmanship; its degree of excellence has a great deal to do with the artistic value of the completed work. Too, every craftsman knows that materials play a very large part in how the completed object looks and feels. For example, a thing molded out of sawdust and glue may have exactly the same dimensions as a wood carving, but the two have nothing but the dimensions in common.

And so it is with the traditional embroidery of Mexico and Guatemala. Through many years and many repetitions, the patterns have been shaped to suit the materials, whether the origin can be traced back to the religious

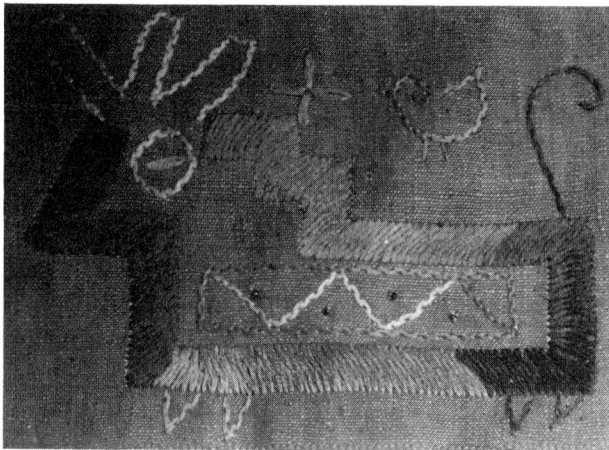

Three examples of modern sophisticated Mexican embroidery. (Collection of the author; photographs: Charles Dorkins)

ideas of preconquest days or only to some Spanish woman's sampler. This fitting of concept to materials has often made almost a new design out of a Spanish or Indian original.

Take a look at these photographs. They show a modern Mexican version of the traditional. The designers, sophisticated people, took the stitches—in this case herringbone and double running stitch—the alternating colors in the outlines, and the tiny birds associated with the larger animal forms, all of which are traditional, and combined them to create new and interesting embroidery. The designers were inspired equally by the traditional and the modern.

Harking back to the repetitions I mentioned, these also have helped to perfect the hand work. A child with nimble fingers learns to cross-stitch. Thirty years later, accurate cross-stitch is second nature, and the mind can be free to work out further variations on the patterns, while the fingers can easily adapt to a change in materials.

Hand-spun and hand-woven textiles have a basic advantage for formalized embroidery. The warp and weft usually have the same dimensions, and it was on this base that Middle American embroidery started. Identical warp and weft make it easier to count the threads. All patterns that are woven involve such counting, and the first embroidery followed suit. Counting was everything, and in many cases still is. In Mayan, xocbichuy—"to count"—is a word for embroidery.

But the materials have undergone a change. Spinning has gone into a decline, and quite a bit of the thread for hand weaving is mass produced, as is the thread for the embroidery itself. In many instances the cotton is the worldwide D.M.C. brand. The silk, which came from China and Spain at one time, is now largely Italian, and it is often replaced by rayon.

Where commercially woven cotton (manta) is the base for embroidery, the designs often become freer, as in servilletas from Magdalena, Guatemala, or blouses from Ocotlán, Oaxaca. The Huichol Indians of Mexico are outstanding for the very fine, very formal, and beautiful symbols they do in cross-stitch on *manta*.

Once the Spanish had consolidated their hold on Middle America, their womenfolk followed, and soon after came the nuns. Embroidery was highly popular in Spain at that time, and the nuns held classes for the Spanish ladies and their creole daughters. European stitchery spread to the house servants, and then to the humbler folk, often changing in form so completely that its relationship to the original European work could not be recognized.

Mexico has several traditional costumes that are definitely of mixed ancestry. They are widely known throughout the country, perhaps better than many that are more clearly of preconquest origin. One of these

A Tehuana in fiesta costume.

is the famed and beautiful fiesta costume of the Tehuanas—the majestic women of the tropical Isthmus of Tehuantepec—with its overall embroidery of roses on velvet, in ombre silk or rayon. Only recently vanished are the felt sombreros of the Tehuantepec men, embroidered in the gold and silver thread known as bullion.

The costume of the Chiapaneca, the mestizo woman of Chiapa de Corzo, is also embroidered with roses, but this time on net. It is an elegant version of the everyday clothing of the area, whose cut is clearly more Spanish than Indian.

In several scattered areas the Indian women have abandoned the *huipil* for the blouse, which they usually embroider in a free style. The becoming blouses from Ocotlán, with their tiny flowers and birds, are now popular all over the world, as the women of that town produce them in quantity for the trade.

The costume of Yucatán changed in a different way. The whole female population,

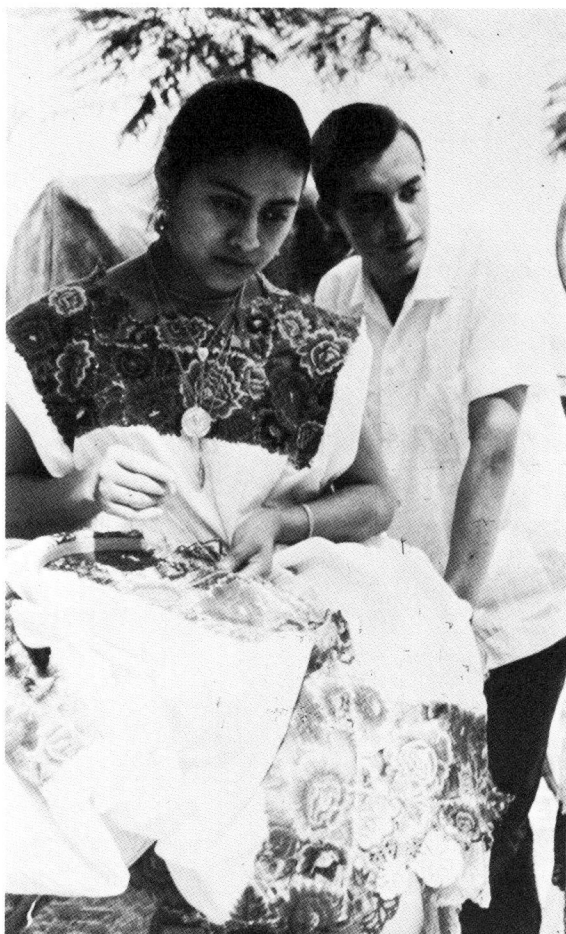

A Mayan woman from Yucatán embroidering a *huipil.* (Photograph: Mexican National Tourist Council)

35

Woman from Ocotlán, state of Oaxaca, Mexico.

Finally, there is the *china poblana*, often the companion of the *charro*, the glamorous Mexican cowboy. Her costume is said to have been invented by a Chinese princess who was carried to Mexico as a captive. Worn at a ceremony, it is a national symbol. It is a melange of everything: red skirt, off-the-shoulder blouse, the national emblem of eagle and cactus embroidered in sequins, the Spanish ruffles and rebozo. It is more Spanish than Indian, apart from the emblem and colors, but not truly Spanish, either. In fact, it is an example of how new materials and new ideas can create a tradition of their own. Perhaps the *china poblana* is truly Mexico!

Spanish and mestizo as well as the native Mayan Indians, wears the *huipil*; long, straight, and cool, it is well suited to the hot climate. The Yucatán *huipil* is edged at neck, sleeves, and hem with embroidery. Since the cut is the same for rich and poor, the well-to-do women could keep a step ahead only by wearing *huipils* that excelled in fabric and workmanship. Some even had theirs made in Paris. The Metropolitan Museum of Art has one of these in its collection, of the finest linen with bands of petit-point pink roses around the neck and hem. It is in a fitting resting place.

The factory age has come to Yucatán, however. Its present-day *huipils* are often made of a fabric that is 50 per cent cotton and 50 per cent polyester, or something similar, and embroidered by machine. But some few are still hand-woven from cotton, and some borders are still decorated by hand.

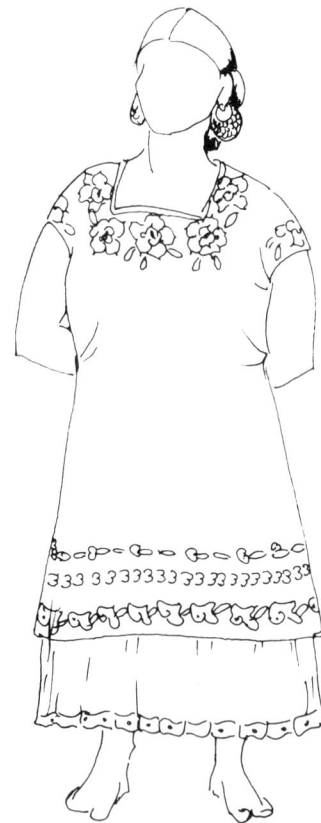

Yucatán woman in long *huipil*.

China poblana.

Cross-stitch and Herringbone Stitch

The Huichols, who live in the harsh mountains of west-central Mexico, do delicate cross-stitch. At one time the fabric was hand-woven cotton, but now it is mostly the unbleached muslin called *manta*. The *manta* and usually the hand-woven cotton have warp and weft of the same weight. Of about the grade that might be called sheeting in the United States, this *manta* is tightly woven and fairly fine, and it is probably washed and bleached before it is used. An ordinary embroidery thread is employed, in one or two strands. The colors are mostly red and blue, with occasional green, lighter blue, and yellow.

Although the figures of men, animals, birds, flowers, and the eight-pointed cross do not appear too unusual, they have special magical meanings to the Huichols. See colorplates 5–8. This is also true of the many purely decorative little bags, without openings, that they wear on a string around their waists. The bigger bags, illustrated separately, do have openings and are used to carry anything from magic potions to money.

The Huichol man is a far grander sight than the woman. Relatively tall and lanky, with his shirt, pants, and the kerchief over his shoulders all embroidered, hung here and there with bags, and carrying a staff, he is a presence.

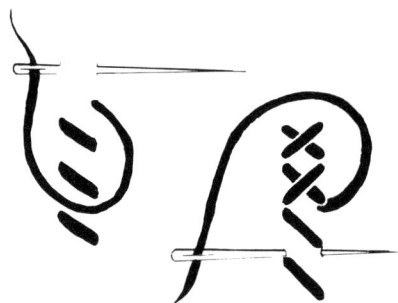

Cross-stitch

Open herringbone stitch

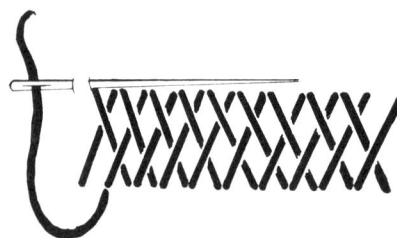

Closed herringbone stitch

Huichol bags showing all-over patterns. (Courtesy, Fondo Nacional para el Fomento Artesanal, Mexico City; photograph: Charles Dorkins)

Another Huichol bag. (Ruth Erickson collection; photograph: Charles Dorkins)

A string of small Huichol bags. (Ruth Erickson collection; photograph: Charles Dorkins)

Huichol embroidery displaying a variety of forms.
(Ruth Erickson collection; photograph:
Charles Dorkins)

The Huichols have a reputation for untidiness, but on occasion they can achieve sartorial elegance. Once in Guadalajara I was visiting the government palace of the state of Jalisco, a magnificent Churrigueresque colonial structure with strong Orozco murals. I glanced around and saw a group or seven or eight Huichols, in their splendid best, who had come to see the governor on tribal business. This was Mexico—colonial magnificence, bold frescoes proclaiming freedom, and the heirs of a preconquest people.

The Huichols retain many of the customs of their ancestors. They are the group that goes on long pilgrimages to fetch the peyote that they use in ritual ceremonies of hallucinations and divining. Their meticulous embroidery almost never employs any stitch but the cross-stitch. In fact, the seams of their garments, when not done by machine, are rather casual.

The cross-stitch appears in many parts of Mexico, but the other section where it pre-

dominates is the Sierra de Puebla, a mountainous area east of Mexico City which includes part of the state of Puebla, plus bits of other states. Its Indians are of several language groups, Otomi, Nahua, Mazahua, Mazatec, and Totonac. Some related nearby peoples outside the Sierra, including the Huastec, also favor cross-stitch. But each group's work has its own individuality.

The cross-stitch of this Sierra has many more variations than the Huichols' work. It is most often done with wool, sometimes on hand-woven wool fabric. Both the designs themselves and their arrangement indicate their origin. Among the designs are the "tree of life" (almost always growing from a pot), the *"flor de piña"* (another bush, usually more open), vines, birds, animals, butterflies, and bugs. See colorplates 9 and 10.

Since this area is heavily populated and within easy reach of Mexico City by road, its

Huichol man

hand work has been heavily exploited for the tourist and gift trade. As a consequence, some of the pieces on sale in the local markets—the town of Huauchinango has the largest—do not have high standards. A good many do, however. My hope is that the salability of the work will encourage the women to go on producing it, and that the demands of the buyers will help to restore the quality where it has slipped.

Cross-stitch and herringbone stitch are the principal ingredients of the examples illustrated, with a few bits of outline stitch.

An older Mexican bag. Note the spirals in the pattern. (Ruth Erickson collection; photograph: Charles Dorkins)

An older bag, most likely Otomi, from the state of Mexico. Fabric is commercial white cotton, but the embroidery is done in hand-spun, home-dyed wool. It is all cross-stitch except the tendrils. Colors are mostly red, with light navy blue. Note that, as often happens, the design is not centered on the bag, which is about ten by fifteen inches.

A recent bag, Otomi work from the state of Mexico, made for the market. Hand-woven from commercially spun and dyed shocking-pink wool. The embroidery, done in wool

Compare this modern bag with the previous one. Both are the work of Otomi Indians from the state of Mexico. (Courtesy, Fondo Nacional para el Fomento Artesanal, Mexico City; photograph: Charles Dorkins)

thread the same weight as in the fabric, is all cross-stitch, with yellow cross-hatching and units in red, orange, purple, and green. Again the pattern is not centered. The bag is twelve by fifteen inches.

A *quechquemitl* from the Huastec area a little northeast of the Sierra de Puebla, where the climate is pleasantly warm. This *quech-*

Note the foliated cross on this *quechquemitl* from the Huastec area of Mexico. (Courtesy, Museo Nacional de Antropologia, Mexico City; photograph: Charles Dorkins)

Observe the edges of this *quechquemitl*; it is Mazahua work from Mexico. (Courtesy, Museo Nacional de Antropologia, Mexico City; photograph: Charles Dorkins)

quemitl is hand-spun and hand-woven of white cotton, and it is embroidered in very fine stitches of gold and terra-cotta commercial thread. The fringe is handmade of the same embroidery cotton, with these colors alternating about every inch and a half, and is whipped onto the edge. The center front is pictured here, with an elaborate cross about seven inches long and a *flor de piña* on each side.

A Mazahua *quechquemitl* from the Sierra, a quite discreet hand-woven garment of navy blue wool. The pattern is white, done with embroidery thread, all in cross-stitch. Note especially the tiny white design on the edges and down the seam below the shoulder. The beautiful finish of this garment is characteristic of the best work of the region.

Servilleta from San Pablito (Little St. Paul), one of the Sierra de Puebla villages famous for the quality of their hand work. This napkin, about ten inches square, was made for ceremonial use. The fabric is hand-woven from white commercial cotton thread. The border is red, as is the central figure, and the birds in the corners are royal blue. The work is very carefully done, with an excellent example of the two-headed eagle. San Pablito has another, more unusual craft. The people make paper from bark, and this is often cut into symmetrical patterns of trees, plants, and animals that are symbols of fertility. Now much of the paper is painted with cheerful designs, a popular tourist item.

Cubierto (cover) about twenty-four by thirty-two inches. This Mazahua product

Mexican *servilleta* includes a two-headed eagle. (Courtesy, Fondo Nacional para el Fomento Artesanal, Mexico City; photograph: Charles Dorkins)

Tablecloth with a stunning all-over pattern. (Courtesy, Fondo Nacional para el Fomento Artesanal, Mexico City; photograph: Charles Dorkins)

shows the same restraint and perfection as the *quechquemitl* described before. It is new and evidently made for sale. The fabric is hand-spun, hand-woven, natural-colored wool; the solid pattern, in herringbone throughout, is in black and golden brown natural wool. The edges are beautifully done in Holbein stitch arabesque.

Colchón (bedspread), perhaps Otomi. Woven from home-dyed purple wool to a width of twenty-eight inches on a treadle loom and sewn down the center to a finished size of fifty-six by eighty-eight inches. Quite probably made to be sold. Embroidered in wool, the quadrilateral pattern is "modern," embodying some forms from embroidery books. But the maker had a good deal of tradition built into her. The tree of life and the *flor de piña* predominate. The people are conventional, as are the birds-with-a-heart. The work is of the proper scale for the area. The stitches are nearly all of the cross-stitch variety, no matter how deformed. The single

lines are done with alternate threads of Holbein stitch and thus look the same on front and back. This is a good example of mestizo work, merging two cultures (page 44).

The table cover shown on colorplates 11 and 12 is Mazahua work, about three by four feet. Hand-spun and hand-loomed cotton, it is embroidered in commercial cotton thread in red, red brown, and black. Each deer is about seven inches long. We have both front and back photographs to show that the finished work is neat and to emphasize the parallel lines on the back of the Holbein stitch. Note the outlines of the animals. The centers of the animals are not cross-stitch, but Holbein zigzag with a running stitch down the center. When accurately spaced, the stitches give the effect of hexagons. Here we have the double cross, an ancient symbol which could be adapted into an eight-pointed star, which pleased the Spanish conquerors more than the double cross. The bottom row of quadrupeds with songbirds (or perhaps

43

One-quarter of a Mexican bedspread, showing how the proportions of the design are adjusted to the overall size. (Collection of the author; photograph: Charles Dorkins)

ibises) above and ducks below is a lovely border. Again notice the border of arabesques in Holbein, which gives the piece a professional finish. These women are adept at borders. They wear three or four full petticoats, each a bit shorter than the next, so that each embroidered border shows. If a petticoat wears out, the border is removed and sewn on a new one.

Blouse from Chiapas, in far southern Mexico. The fabric is commercial *manta*, and the cross-stitch embroidery is in commercial thread in red, light blue, black, pink, and yellow. This area has many coffee plantations whose workers came from other sections and have largely forgotten their traditions. Most recently, many of these farms have been handed over to the workers as *ejidos*, to be operated communally in an ancient Mexican form of land use. Returning to the blouse, its yoke was embroidered separately, with the body attached later by simple overcasting, leaving a tiny free pleat. The shoulder ruffle is similarly attached, and the photograph reveals the reverse of the ruffle edging.

Note how the body is attached to the yoke of this blouse from the state of Chiapas in Mexico. (Courtesy, Fondo Nacional para el Fomento Artesanal, Mexico City; photograph: Charles Dorkins)

44

Huipil from Bochil, Chiapas. Another example from an area where tradition has almost evaporated. But this time there is a modern ornament on traditional fabric, red-striped and hand-woven in a rectilinear shape. The embroidery is accurate cross-stitch of pink, red, and purple, with the diamond shapes in blue, yellow, and green. The square neckline is buttonholed in a variety of colors.

The design on this portion of a *huipil* from Bochil, Chiapas, is very geometric. (Courtesy, Fondo Nacional para el Fomento Artesanal, Mexico City; photograph: Charles Dorkins)

Embroidery on the armhole of the same *huipil* is much more inventive. (Courtesy, Fondo Nacional para el Fomento Artesanal, Mexico City; photograph: Charles Dorkins)

Below is the armhole of the previous *huipil.* The pattern of birds and plants is much more open and inventive than the neckline, but it is embroidered in similar colors. The hole is edged with buttonhole stitching. I doubt that both neck and armholes were done by the same person.

A *huipil* from Valle Nacional. (Courtesy, Museo Nacional de Antropologia, Mexico City; photograph: Charles Dorkins)

Huipils from Valle Nacional in the state of Oaxaca. They are large, about fifty-six by forty inches, and are made in three pieces (observe the embroidered seams). The fabric is hand-spun and hand-woven with an openwork pattern. The embroidery is cross-stitch, mostly in red and blue. The patterns are not indigenous, but may have been taken from something like an embroidery book or

A *huipil* from Valle Nacional, in Mexico. The embroiderer used the whole pattern book! (Ruth Erickson collection; photograph: Charles Dorkins)

a calendar. Many flights of fancy have been achieved in the process, however, and the workmanship is good, making a stunning effect. In both *huipils* the top center front is solid cross-stitch. One has spirals, the other diamonds; undoubtedly this solid part was a feature of the traditional *huipil* of the area.

Blouse from the Zoques near Chiapa de Corzo, state of Chiapas. From this blouse grew the fancy "Chiapaneca" costume, all black net ruffles with colored satin-stitched flowers. In this example, the net ruffle is done that way and edged with buttonhole. The neckline has fine cross-stitch holding the gathers and imitating the embroidered ribbon in its pattern.

A Zoque blouse, very Spanish in feeling. (Courtesy, Fondo Nacional para el Fomento Artesanal, Mexico City; photograph: Charles Dorkins)

Satin Stitch and Related Work

Satin stitch

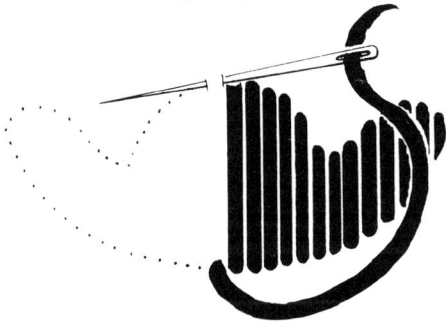

False satin stitch

Holbein stitch A

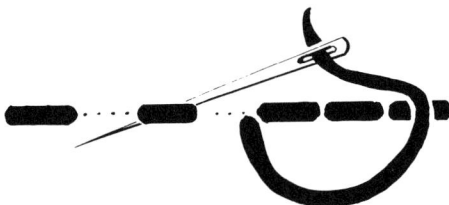

Holbein stitch B

In these countries, satin stitch is most often the surface type, in which the needle catches just a thread at the edge of the outline and crosses again to the other side. Obviously, this saves almost half the thread required for the normal satin stitch.

This stitch frequently appears in combination with others, including Holbein, flat, feather, stem, or outline stitches. In the first example it is used alone.

Flat stitch

Feather stitch

Stem stitch

The all-over roses of the Tehuantepec fiesta costume. (Ruth Erickson collection; photograph: Charles Dorkins)

From a *huipil* worn in Ixtatán, Guatemala. (Courtesy, University of Pennsylvania Museum; photograph: Charles Dorkins)

This is part of the all-over pattern of the much-admired Tehuantepec fiesta *huipil*. The whole costume of Mexico's Tehuanas, comprising *huipil* and skirt, is black velvet solidly embroidered in shaded roses. There is no formal repeat, just one rose next to another. The effect requires the availability of embroidery cotton in many gradations of color. It is obviously patterned after the traditional Spanish shawl, which came originally from China, but the Tehuanas have successfully made it their own.

A portion of a long *huipil*—perhaps forty-five inches wide and thirty-six inches long—from San Mateo Ixtatán, Guatemala. The pattern is twenty-five inches from center of neck to point. The fabric is muslin, and the solid embroidery, predominantly in red, is done with the commercial cotton thread that is sold in hanks in Guatemala for weaving. This thread is not as tightly twisted as proper embroidery thread, so it has no sheen. It is also finer, so several threads are used at once, giving the appearance of being built up and producing a thick and heavy garment. The sun symbol falls on the chest and is repeated on each side and the back. The whole pattern radiates from the neck opening. It is a tremendous amount of work for a highly dramatic effect. Note that there is no space between the concentric bands.

One pattern from a large *huipil*, this comes from Huautla de Jiménez, a mountain village southeast of Puebla. The seams joining the three strips of fabric are covered with red and blue ribbon. The design shown here falls on the chest and is about fourteen inches wide. It too has been embroidered with the red commercial cotton intended for weaving. The fabric is woven by hand in a slightly openwork style with white thread of the same type. The prominent bird in the all-red pattern is an eagle. Huautla means "place of the eagle," and the village is the center of the cult that employs hallucinogenic mushrooms in its religious rites. The embroidery is done in surface satin stitch, with flat stitch where the spaces are too wide to use satin. The edges are mostly worked in outline stitch to provide a strong, clean silhouette.

Huipil from Huautla de Jiménez, "place of the eagle." (Courtesy, Metropolitan Museum of Art, New York; photograph: Charles Dorkins)

Child's *huipil* from Soyaltepec, Oaxaca, thirty-two by twenty-six inches. It is embroidered on *manta* in red and peach, mostly in surface satin stitch with flat stitch in the longer spaces. These are lovely birds that I consider suitable for adaptation (see photograph on page 50).

Colorplate 14 is from a man's short pants from Santiago Atitlán, Guatemala. This is hand-woven cloth with a red vertical stripe and various-colored horizontal stripes. The tiny figures, an inch to an inch and a quarter high, are called *muñecas*, or dolls, the Spanish name given to any small figure. Notice how accurately they are placed by counting threads. A similar effect could be created—and often is—by finger weaving, but the women of Atitlán prefer to embroider. The *muñecas* are in satin stitch and so are the quetzals—the long-tailed national bird—in a very free way. Stem stitch makes the single-line arms and legs. The herringbone design is the maker's signature. The colors, bright and casually arranged, are red, yellow, lavender, and dark green.

49

From Soyaltepec, Mexico, a *huipil* for a child. (Courtesy, Fondo Nacional para el Fomento Artesanal, Mexico City; photograph: Charles Dorkins)

A quarter of a skirt of an obsolete type once used by the Totonacs of the Papantla area in east-central Mexico. It is white hand-woven cotton embroidered in two shades of blue, probably indigo. The embroidery is true satin stitch in a geometric form, except for the cross-stitch seams. The design is reminiscent of Spanish work.

Colorplate 13 shows a *huipil* from Santa María Sacatepequez in Guatemala, of hand-woven heavy white cotton. This pretty front and a bit on the armholes are the entire decoration. The blocks are all surface satin stitch and are divided diagonally into trian-

gular quarters of different colors, including red, orange, yellow, pink, navy blue, and green. Some of the *muñecas* are in cross-stitch, some in satin stitch. The neckline is finished simply with buttonhole work.

Next is part of the skirt from Chilapa, in the state of Guerrero on Mexico's Pacific slope. It is basically of hand-woven, indigo-dyed navy blue cotton, about two and a half yards by thirty-eight inches. Three stripes of light blue run the long way of the cloth, with the widest stripe nearest the selvedge. These stripes are then embroidered with silk or rayon. The concept seems to be derived

Detail of an old Totonac Indian skirt from Mexico. (Courtesy, Museo Nacional de Antropologia, Mexico City; photograph: Charles Dorkins)

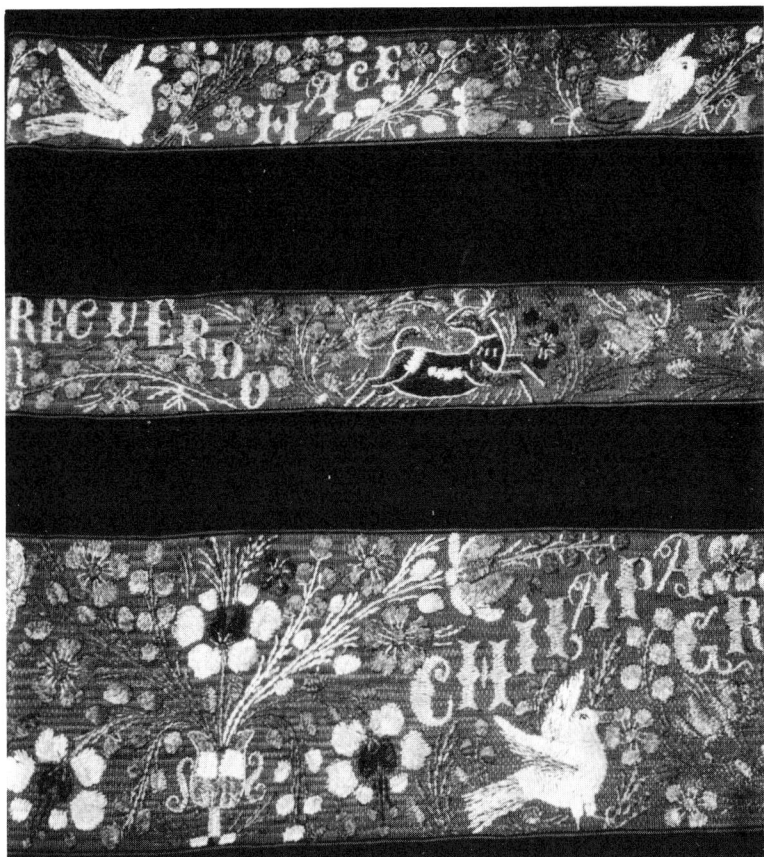

The name of Chilapa, where it was made, is embroidered onto this Mexican skirt. (Ruth Erickson collection; photograph: Charles Dorkins)

from the flower-brocaded ribbon that is still imported from Europe. But the patterns are the embroiderer's own, consisting of local animals, birds, and flowers, sometimes with lettering. The colors are light and lively, and the work is all satin stitch or outline stitch.

A Guatemalan *huipil* neckline, this one from San Mateo Ixtatán, Huehuetenango, probably an everyday garment. It is all satin stitch, largely in reds and yellows. Note the horizontal band all the way across the chest. The neckline is reminiscent of the sun's rays. Most engaging are the birds and little figures.

The *muñecas* on colorplate 15, mostly birds (there might be a cat), are from the front of a man's pants of Zacatepec, Mexico. The big-

Neckline of a Guatemalan *huipil* from San Mateo Ixtatán. (Courtesy, University of Pennsylvania Museum; photograph: Charles Dorkins)

Collar produced by a
Guatemalan cottage industry.
(Courtesy, Metropolitan
Museum of Art, New York;
photograph: Charles Dorkins)

gest is about an inch high. Most are satin stitch, though an occasional cross-stitch shows up. The pant legs, incidentally, have a handsome drawn-work hem. The material is hand-spun and hand-loomed.

This is a quarter of a round ruffled collar that is the product of an unusual Guatemalan cottage industry. It was produced in San Francisco el Alto, one of the places that make other communities' traditional clothing. This collar is part of the women's costume of the nearby town of Totonicapán and was taken there to be sold in the market. Similarly, skirt textiles are often woven centrally, and other bits of traditional wear also are produced. This particular collar, which is to be worn over a white blouse, is worked in

fine false satin stitch and outline stitch. The wreaths are in lavender, the flowers in yellow and purple. Lavender is a favorite color in the Guatemalan highlands, and many garments have just a bit here and there. It may represent a memory of the purple of the murex, which was rare and precious when available long ago.

The *huipil* from Ocotlán, in the Mexican state of Oaxaca, that is portrayed in colorplate 16 is one of the most popular tourist souvenirs. It is long and slightly full and makes a pretty dress. It is made of good commercially woven cloth, and the embroidery usually is excellently done. The little flowers are mostly in reds and pinks, with dark green leaves, all in satin stitch and stem

"Make me if you can" is the name
of this work from Ocotlán, Mexico.
(Courtesy, Fondo Nacional para el
Fomento Artesanal, Mexico City;
photograph: Charles Dorkins)

stitch. The yoke, sleeve cape, and underarm facing are embroidered separately and assembled later. The edges are then beautifully finished with needle lace. The really outstanding work is the band of embroidery —actually smocking—used to hold the gathers at the yoke in front and back, illustrated here. This band is five-eighths of an inch wide and features a row of tiny figures. The background is done first in stem stitch, leaving space for the figures. These are filled in with satin stitch, leaving faces blank on the females and arms blank on the males. This work is called *hazme si puedes*—"make me if you can"—which neatly expresses the challenge it presents. It requires a remarkable combination of sharp eyesight and physical coordination. The local diet must contain ample vitamin A.

A *huipil* neckline from Quezaltenango, Guatemala, another version inspired by imported ribbon. This time it is done in artificial silk on a heavily brocaded *huipil* and is used as a neck finish. The blue flowers with white centers and the green leaves are satin stitch, while the background is filled solidly with stem stitch. The whole is about two inches wide.

This smocklike blouse is from an area in Chiapas where the people have lost their traditional roots through migration. The embroidered yoke is competently done in bands of red satin-stitch flowers, plus three bands of double herringbone. The gathers are neatly held by rows of stem stitch—almost smocking.

A beautiful *quechquemitl* from Pautepec, Puebla, is displayed on a mannequin as it

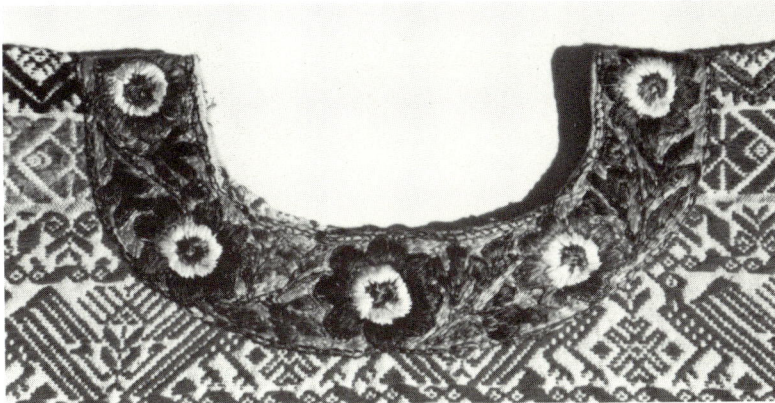

Another example of embroidery inspired by ribbon, this one from Guatemala. (Courtesy, Metropolitan Museum of Art, New York; photograph: Charles Dorkins)

Blouse from Aguatenango, in Mexico's southern state of Chiapas. (Courtesy, Fondo Nacional para el Fomento Artesanal, Mexico City; photograph: Charles Dorkins)

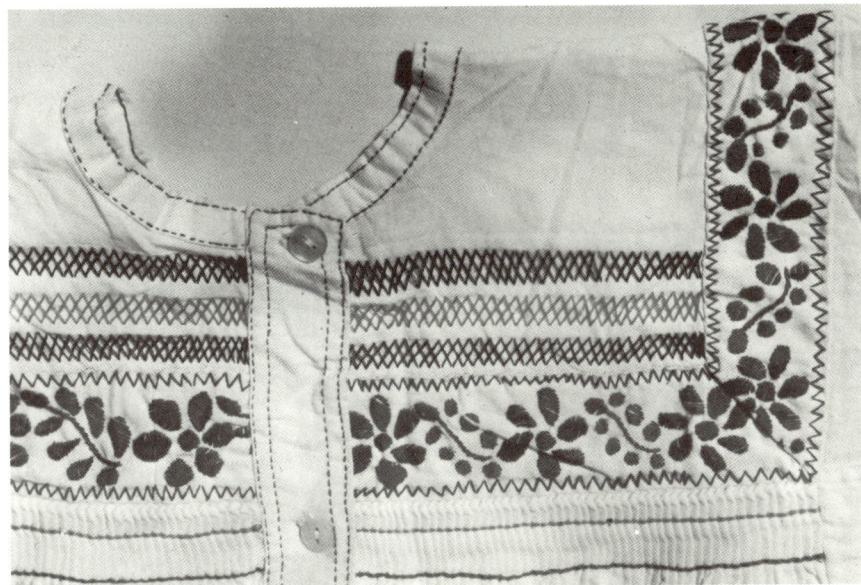

Mexican *quechquemitl* with both embroidered and woven designs.
(Courtesy, Museo Nacional de Antropologia, Mexico City;
photograph: Charles Dorkins)

would be worn. The designs are both woven
and embroidered. The broad band of bold
double spirals, a snake symbol, is brocade
woven in heavy wool on white cotton. The
square at center front above it is embroidered. Done in a way that leaves some of the
white background showing, the embroidery
is heavy wool satin stitch and is floral in
character. The background of the woven
hexagons is red and gold. The embroidery
is mostly reds and pinks, with some yellow
and dark blue.

✺ Unusual Combinations ✺

These five pieces defy classification because they display an assortment of stitches, but all are unusual work.

A *servilleta* from Magdalena, Guatemala, about twenty-two by twenty-eight inches. It is made of *manta* and embroidered in red cotton with an occasional spray of lavender. The pompoms are chain stitch, each stitch radiating from the center (once called lazy daisy), and the stems are stem stitch. Note the interesting all-over pattern the woman achieved. It should be fun to do this one.

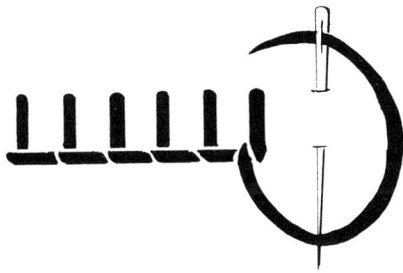

Buttonhole stitch A

Chain stitch

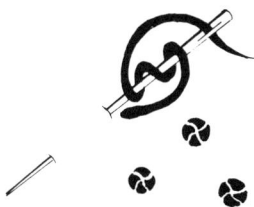

French knots

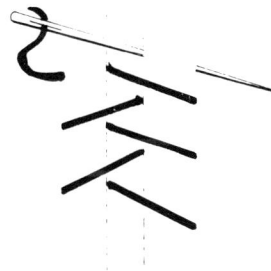

Lacing

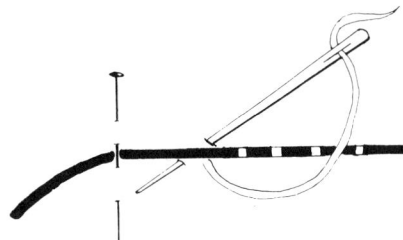

Couching

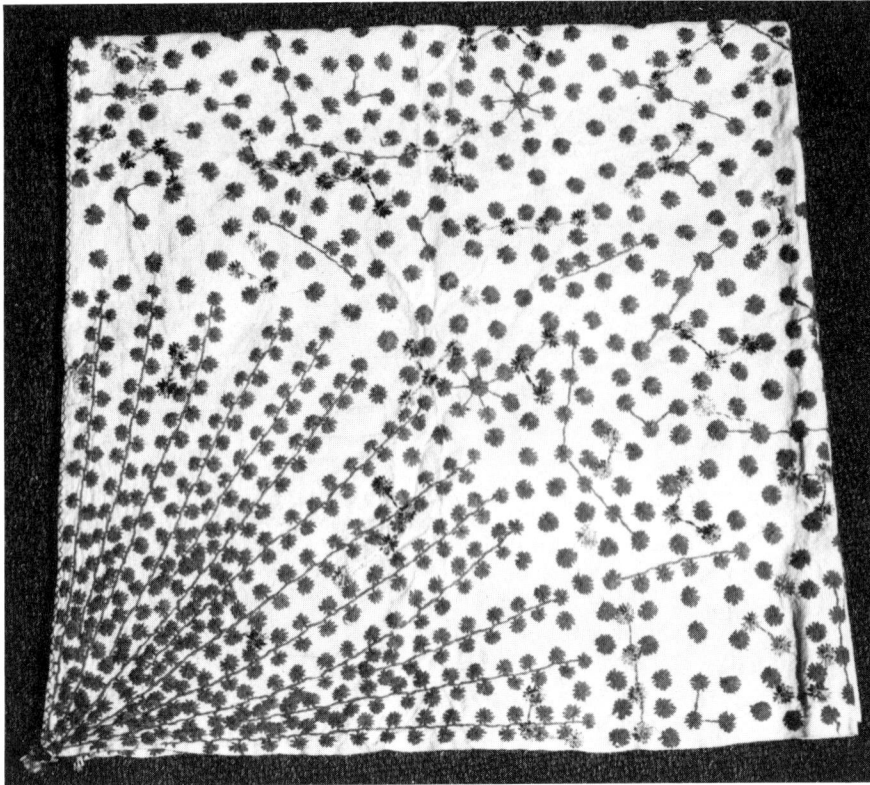

Servilleta from Magdalena, Guatemala. (Courtesy, University of Pennsylvania Museum; photograph: Charles Dorkins)

Otomi bedspread with a variety of stitches. (Museo Nacional de Antropologia, Mexico City; photograph: Charles Dorkins)

A Mexican *quechquemitl* with openwork. (Courtesy, Museo Nacional de Antropologia, Mexico City; photograph: Charles Dorkins)

This is a *colchón* (bedspread) from the Otomi area north of Mexico City. It is heavy wool woven in a simple plaid pattern of dark red and black. The embroidery is done with quite heavy, well-twisted cotton in a double strand, and the versatility is notable. The chevrons are satin stitch, the little branches chain stitch. Cross-stitch is used in the filled squares. The daisylike flowers are concentric chain, and the starlike flowers are similar, but with fewer petals and a long stitch to make their points. The cross is buttonhole and outline stitch. And all is worked to fit the background squares.

The *quechquemitl* with white openwork is from Cuetzalán, a Nahua village in Puebla. It is undecorated except for the visible corner, which is embroidered mostly in red, orange, and pink. The seams are in outline stitch with sequins at the ends. The heavier lines at the base are long and short buttonhole, and lacing stitch. There are tassels at the corners. Double zigzag makes the upper curve. This pattern owes its distinctiveness to the open-weave background.

Colorplate 17 shows the corner of a *quech-quemitl* from Tancanhuitz, state of San Luis Potosi, in northeast Mexico. The design is in green, red, orange, and pink wool on hand-loomed cotton. There are familiar symbols; the tree of life, *flor de piña*, a cross, and two attractive birds. The outstanding fact here is that the design is couched. The couching is so close together that the couched thread is almost completely covered. The small, more open areas are worked in French knots. The fringe is homemade and attached with chain stitch. In all, a vibrant effect.

From the Mixtec area of Mexico, another

This unusual Mixtec work from the state of Oaxaca combines pile with French knots. (Ruth Erickson collection; photograph: Charles Dorkins)

57

combination of unusual weaving with embroidery. The solid strips are woven in red and black wool. The woolen weft is carefully "picked up" between each two warp threads, a filler is put through behind the loops thus formed, and the whole is battened down. Pile is the end result. The more open strips with the diamond-shaped figures are thousands of French knots; the fabric is hand-spun cotton, rather heavy and certainly closely woven.

Running, Darning, Overcasting, and Other Simple Stitches

Running stitch

We start with two belts from Guatemala, in colorplate 19, and one from Mexico, pictured on page 26, which are all very similar. The belts are of very heavy cotton thread with black edge stripes, and the widest belt has two black interior stripes. These stripes add sparkle to the finished work. The embroidery is done with heavy, tightly twisted wool. The stitch is called "running," but in this case it must have been more like laborious trudging, pushing down and up, down and up, with a heavy needle. We show the backs of the belts, too. All these are more than six feet long and go around the wearer several times. They probably would take many years to wear out.

Two tops for *huipils* from the Sierra de Puebla (page 60), probably from Caucuila, a village whose embroidery is marketed in Huauchinango or some other center, with the buyer either incorporating it into a garment or reselling it. The white cotton fabric, called *empaque*, is woven especially for embroidery, with the warp and weft identical and a bit heavy, like a fine-grade monk's cloth. The threads are very easy to count. The body of these garments is *manta*. The embroidery is done in red mercerized cotton in running stitch, with the narrow diagonals in overcasting. The crocheted edges were put on last.

A made-for-market *huipil* top from the Sierra de Puebla. (Collection of the author; photograph: Charles Dorkins)

A *tzut*, the ceremonial cloth from Chichicastenango in Guatemala, used and made by men, is pictured in colorplate 20. The material is red with black pinstripes about half an inch apart. This gives an idea of the size of the design, which is worked in minute and exact overcasting. The proportion is more like petit point, but the stitches are vertical rather than diagonal. Sometimes a *tzut* is almost solid embroidery. This is probably the most outstanding type of work done in these countries. It is done with untwisted silk and glows like jewels. The humpbacked horse is a familiar figure in this region's work, and so are the healthy chickens. At the left side, the diagonal multilegged cross.

The designs from a large *huipil* made in Ojitlán, Oaxaca, shown on the facing page, with a detail in colorplate 21, are done in red untwisted cotton on white open-weave hand-loomed fabric. You can see how the upside-down-headed bird fits into the space between selvedges; it is quite big, maybe ten inches across. Above is our old acquaintance the snake, with a bit of lightning. The peacock is splendid. They are all done with

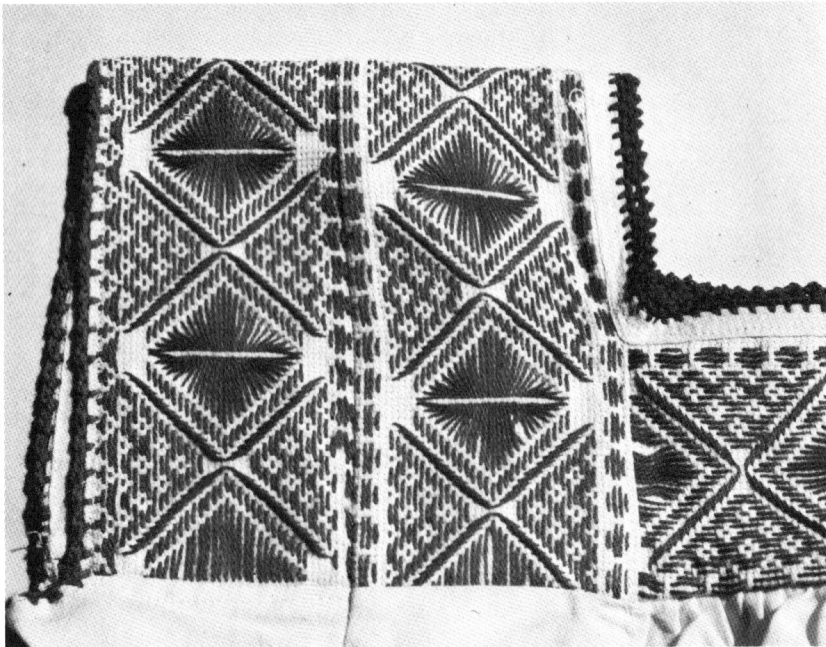

Another example of a made-for-market *huipil* top. (Courtesy, Fondo Nacional para el Fomento Artesanal, Mexico City; photograph: Charles Dorkins)

The bird with the twisted neck is from Ojitlán, in Mexico's state of Oaxaca.
(Courtesy, Fondo Nacional para el Fomento Artesanal, Mexico City;
photograph: Charles Dorkins)

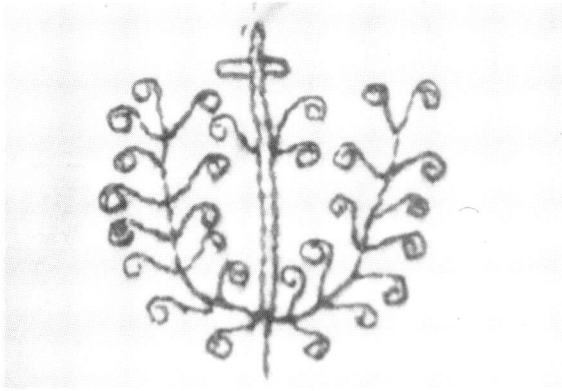

Wreath from a Mexican man's shirt. (Courtesy, Museo Nacional de Antropologia, Mexico City; photograph: Charles Dorkins)

running stitch; a few threads of blue and yellow are introduced among the red in order to keep the pattern from being perfect. The designs seem preconquest.

The little wreath in black Holbein appears at the base of the placket of a man's white hand-woven shirt. It is about five by five inches. From Huistán, Mexico.

In colorplate 22 is a finely woven *huipil* of commercial cotton thread, from Xochistlahuaca, in the Mexican state of Guerrero. Like some others, it has a handsome woven pattern that leaves a space for the embroidered zigzag (which the weaver could just as easily have inserted on the loom). The zigzag, in bands of red, orange, blue, and green cotton, is worked in running stitch and is positioned by counting the fabric's threads.

A *huipil* from Mexico's Mixtec region, woven in white in alternate stripes of solid and nettinglike weaves. The contrasting net gives the stripes a seersucker look. The pattern is simply darned in wool, much heavier than the background thread.

Another *servilleta* or *tzut* from Chichicastenango is shown in colorplate 18. It is worked in overcasting—like petit point—on tightly hand-woven white cotton with beige stripes. Animals and figures are in red, with small yellow and blue embellishments. The figures used are traditional symbols of fertility, and this *tzut* was probably used ceremonially for carrying seed corn. (Note the well-done *randa*.)

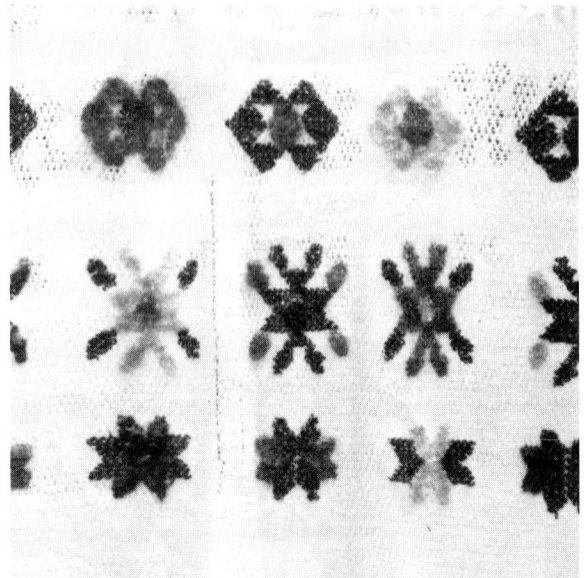

Huipil from the Mixtec area of Oaxaca, Mexico. (Courtesy, Museo Nacional de Antropologia, Mexico City; photograph: Charles Dorkins)

62

✺ Smocking ✺

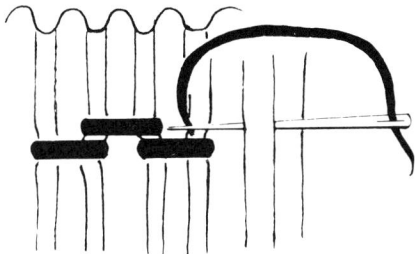

Smocking

Smocking was a European import that did not take very well when grafted onto Indian hand work, but some is done. The idea of putting forth so much effort to pleat and restrain the fullness had little appeal. There were many more possibilities in an embroidered flat yoke or band to whose edge the gathered material could be sewn.

The blouse from Tojobales, Chiapas, is made of *manta* and has a smocked ruffle. The smocking is bold and unconventional, done in satin stitch and herringbone. The pleats were evidently basted down and the embroidery applied to fasten the ruffle to the body of the garment. The hem is finished in a similar fashion, using a row of blue feather stitching and a repeat of the triangular satin-stitch motif, then more feather stitching. An unusual piece.

Also pictured on page 64 is a Mexican blouse, provenance unknown, that is old and a lovely example of classic smocking using stem stitch. The buttonholed, herringboned neckline is particularly nice. The shoulders have flat bands above the armholes. This is black embroidery on white fabric, reminiscent of seventeenth-century Spain.

On page 65 are two excellent examples of Mexican smocking, done on separate pieces to be incorporated later into the finished garments. Also in black on white.

Bold smocking on a blouse from Tojobales in southern Mexico. (Courtesy, Museo Nacional de Antropologia, Mexico City; photograph: Charles Dorkins)

An old Mexican blouse with classic smocking. (Courtesy, Metropolitan Museum of Art, New York; photograph: Charles Dorkins)

Two more examples of Mexican smocking. (Courtesy, Metropolitan Museum of Art, New York; photograph: Charles Dorkins)

A modern blouse, perhaps from the state of Oaxaca, of loosely woven *manta*. There is a yoke, and below it the smocking is about seven inches wide, done in orange cotton thread with tack stitch. This **unusual technique** involves running a thread to catch the peak of every other pleat in alternate rows, and then (where it disappears from sight in the picture) reaching down to catch the bottom of the pleat. The pattern is lively and not traditional.

Unusual smocking technique on a Mexican blouse. (Courtesy, Fondo Nacional para el Fomento Artesanal, Mexico City; photograph: Charles Dorkins)

Fishbone stitch B

Edgings, Seams, and Necklines— Randa, Fishbone, Buttonhole, and Magic Braid

Buttonhole stitch B

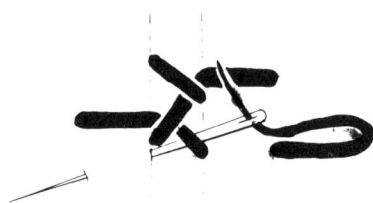
Randa A

Buttonhole stitch C

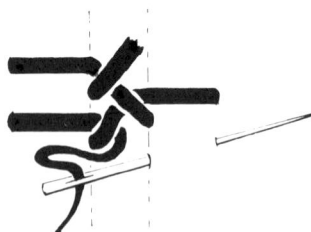
Randa B

Magic braid A

Fishbone stitch A

Magic braid B

The way a garment is finished says something about the person who made it. A good workman wants the total effect to be as nearly perfect as possible, and you can tell that a great many of the Mexican and Guatemalan needlewomen have a justified pride in their skills.

Seams get special attention, and so do necklines, armholes, and sometimes even hems and the ends of plackets. Most of the stitches may not be out of the ordinary, but they are well done and suitable.

Let us begin with the *randa*, mentioned earlier as the one type of embroidery that can be identified in preconquest relics. The word actually is Spanish, literally meaning "lacing" or "lace maker"; it is in general use today, leaving no trace that I can find of the original Indian names for it. I believe the *randa* is a unique technique for fastening two pieces of fabric together edge to edge. It was usually necessary because the hip loom produced fabric that was too narrow, when wrapped around horizontally, to make a long skirt, even though Indian women are short (some in Guatemala are no more than four feet six inches tall).

In making a *randa*, the material is first folded back to make a narrow hem on one edge of each piece. The edges are then placed parallel to each other and are linked with over-and-under stitches, as shown in the diagrams. The result is similar to satin stitch or lacing stitch, with a ridge down the center. It makes an excellent seam because when the threads are caught in this way they act as knots and prevent ripping.

Randa is almost never done in one color, but ordinarily in several alternating colors in sections of a couple of inches each. The width can vary.

The first example, in colorplate 24, is from Zunil, Guatemala. The fabric is basically red, with stripes of two blues, red, yellow, and white clustered together. The dark blue makes the center selvedge. The *randa* is of two widths, and the alternation of the colors makes the finished work stand out. Below the *randa* the seam is buttonholed together,

with the stitches in groups of two on alternating sides, making almost a zigzag effect. The neckline is rolled and closely whipped to form a strong raised edge.

A skirt from Venustiano Carranza, in the Mexican state of Chiapas, pictured in colorplate 25, has a most elaborate arrangement of *randas*, involving both vertical and horizontal seams. These are about four inches wide, plus an added decorative X in satin and stem stitches where the *randas* meet. The fabric is heavy navy blue hand-loomed cotton, and the pattern is in red and gold artificial silk, plus a bit of dark green cotton. When worn, this part of the pattern is at the woman's right rear. The horizontal band runs almost all the way around, except where it would be folded under in the pleats.

The accompanying *huipil*, not pictured, is of a white gauzelike fabric with a white pattern in rows. The various designs have such names as "fishbones," "eggs," and "candy." The men's shirts are of a similar pattern. A gathering of villagers in these costumes gives an effect of great artistry and wealth. The time and materials needed to make them are perhaps available because of Venustiano Carranza's cash crop, a scale insect that secretes lac. This resinous substance is sold in nearby Chiapa de Corzo, where widely known lacquered gourds (*jicaras*) are made.

The decorative seam shown in colorplate 23 is part of a large ceremonial *huipil* from Quezaltenango, Guatemala. The fabric is gauzelike, firmly whipped with lavender cotton, and the dainty sprigs are done with chain stitch, also in lavender.

Shown at the top of page 68 is a handwoven fabric that has a red stripe near the selvedge. The edges are whipped together in alternating red and navy blue. On alternate sides of the seam are little blocks of tiny fishbone stitches in many colors, in quite heavy wool. From Chiapas, Mexico.

The beautiful old *huipil* from Chichicastenango, shown in colorplate 26, is full of symbolism. The neck is outlined in points, for the rays of the sun. Next are the four moon-circles. The pattern is similar to that of

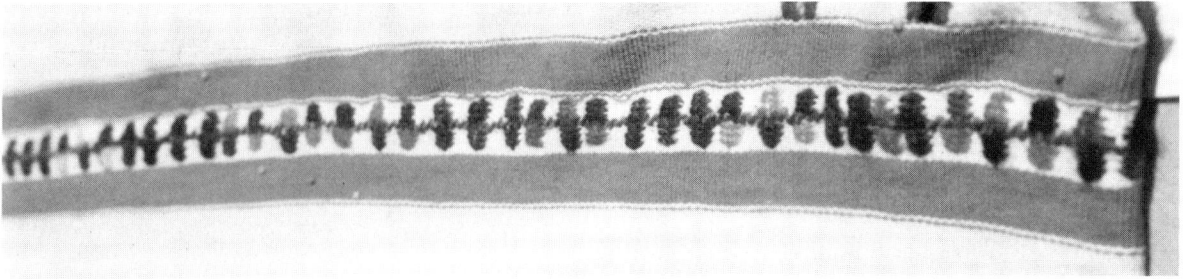

Fishbone stitches on the sides of a seam. (Ruth Erickson collection; photograph: Charles Dorkins)

the famous Aztec calendar stone. The double-headed bird here was perhaps adapted from the emblem of the Hapsburg kings of Spain. Also, there are a woven zigzag (lightning or rain), corn plants on each side, and numerous double crosses. The pattern of decoration itself makes a cross, representing the four cardinal points of the *milpa* or cornfield.

The seams are finished with buttonholing in groups of three, forming zigzags. The neck opening is rolled back and whipped down, and the black taffeta points are sewn in with three rows of chain stitching, red, yellow, and red. Each moon is made of a band of taffeta sewn around the circumference with chain stitch, then gathered to the center and fastened with tiny chain-stitch circles.

Pictured in colorplate 27 is the front of a *huipil* from Sololá, Guatemala, of handsome red-and-white-striped hand-woven cloth. This is a different treatment of the ideas in the previous *huipil*. The neck is bound in pink taffeta, cut into points that are fastened with chain stitching around their edges. The taffeta moon's outer edge is fishbone stitch, and there are concentric circles of Holbein stitch on the taffeta; the center is a tiny open space through which you can just see the underlying fabric. Elsewhere, the heavy concentric circles are fishbone edged with stem

stitch, and all the rays are chain stitch. The effect is that of a necklace. The embroidery is in dark blue, green, gold, and purple silk.

The neckline of a well-done *huipil* from Joyabaj, Guatemala, shown in colorplate 31, has almost lost the symbolism. The fabric is hand-spun, hand-woven navy blue cotton with a very fine red pinstripe. Self-bound, the neckline is surrounded by chain stitch in artificial silk. The concentric circles of embroidery are:

(1) Purple feather stitch
(2) White satin-stitch zigzags
(3) Pale green feather stitch
(4) Gold satin-stitch scallops centered with purple dots
(5) Purple feather stitching
(6) White stems in double chain stitch surrounding flowers of satin stitch, their petals divided by Holbein stitch
(7) Pale green feather stitching
(8) Gold scallops
(9) Purple dots
(10) Green feather stitching
(11) White zigzag

The armholes are similar.

A two-width *huipil* in heavy red hand-woven cotton, in colorplate 29, is from Zum-

The famed Aztec calendar stone. (Photograph: Mexican National Tourist Council)

Note the neckline of this Guatemalan *huipil.*
(Ruth Erickson collection; photograph:
Charles Dorkins)

pango, Guatemala. There is a neat *randa*
down the center, and the neckline is bound
with close, tight buttonhole stitch in purple
enlivened with bits of other colors. All concentric circles are three rows of chain stitch,
successively in green and purple; then
purple, blue, and purple; then purple, white,
and purple. The "rays" are satin stitch, edged
with purple chain stitch, in green, gold, blue,
purple, and white. The flowers are also satin
stitch. The sheaves have stems of chain stitch.
Artificial silk is used for the embroidery.

Huipil from San Pedro Sacatepequez, Guatemala. This has been included to show a

modern example of brocade weaving done in
heavy mercerized cotton of many colors. The
neck is tightly whipped in dark green and
decorated with Holbein-stitch zigzags. Several rows of the same stitch go around the
base. The *randa* is small, neat, and strong.
Not delicate workmanship, but extremely
professional.

Below is one of the edges for the *huipils* of
Merida, Yucatán, that are sold in the market
by the piece, to be attached to garments by
the buyers. Its cross-stitched roses are completely European in style, but they are com-
petent work.

Colorplate 30 pictures a *huipil* from Chichicastenango that is woven of the often-men-
tioned but unusual natural brown cotton. For
the photograph we carefully folded it so that
the brown fabric can be clearly seen through
the neck opening. The neckline has the traditional points and four moon-circles. The
minute overcasting and the chain-stitch embroidery are in purple and gold silk, a very
rich combination with the golden brown fabric. Probably done by a man.

The joining on a *huipil* from Valle Nacional,
Mexico, is done with lacing stitch in alternate
sections of red and navy blue, about two
inches wide.

A simple, well-done *randa* from Yalalag, in
the mountains of the state of Oaxaca in Mexico, in one-and-a-half-inch segments of red,
gold, green, pink, and blue. Note the tiny
central ridge made by the interlacing.

"Magic braid" is what I call the stitch that
finishes the seams on a Sierra de Puebla bag

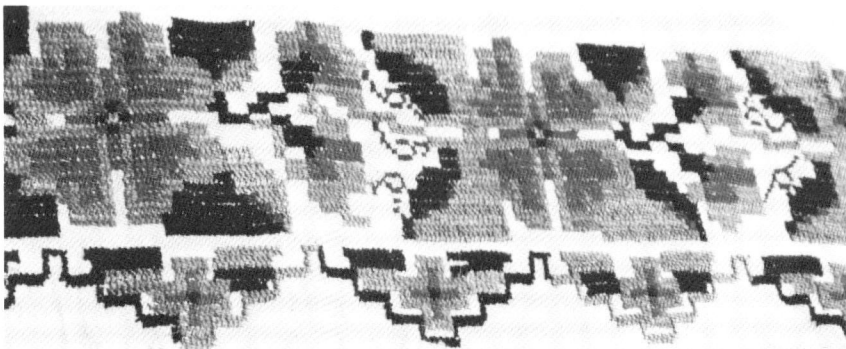

Huipil edging from Yucatán.
(Courtesy, Fondo Nacional
para el Fomento Artesanal,
Mexico City; photograph:
Charles Dorkins)

70

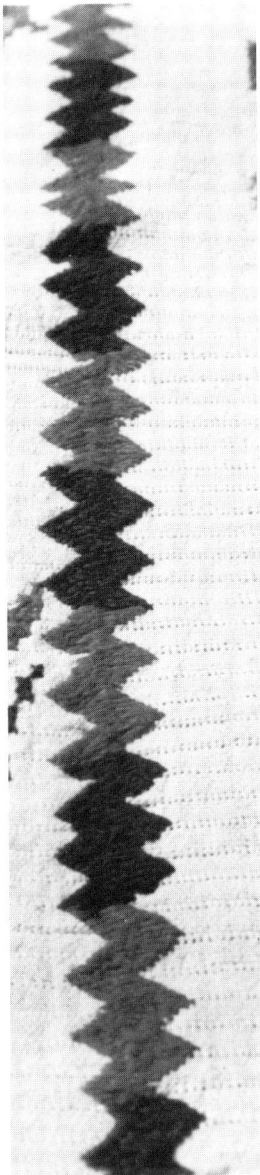

A lacing-stitch joining done in Valle Nacional, Mexico. (Ruth Erickson collection; photograph: Charles Dorkins)

A simple *randa* from Yalalag, in the Oaxaca mountains. (Ruth Erickson collection; photograph: Charles Dorkins)

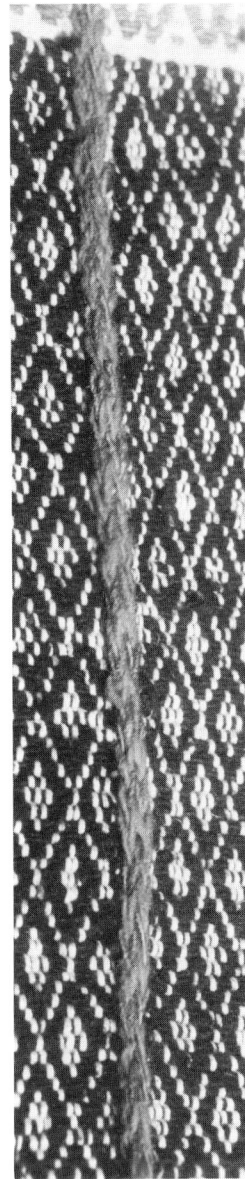

Seam on a bag from Mexico's Sierra de Puebla. (Collection of the author; photograph: Charles Dorkins)

that is hand-woven in black on white in a diaper pattern. The stitch is done in alternating colors of bright pink and lavender wool. The needle is threaded with both colors. Begin as for chain stitch, throwing only *one* thread around the needle (the other color will vanish). Then go over that thread, put the needle in, and go *backward* and bring it out in the center of the loop. Put the needle in the same hole, move forward, and bring it out ahead of the existing loop, and throw the other thread around the needle. Repeat, throwing the first thread around the needle. You will have arrow shapes of alternating colors. Two rows of this stitch side by side will give the effect of interlocking *W*s.

71

Chain Stitch

The remarkable example of chain stitch in colorplate 28 was done by hand. The picture shows one-quarter of an everyday *huipil* from the Tehuantepec area. (Remember the shaded roses on velvet, the Tehuantepec fiesta garb?) The pattern here covers the fabric, which is ordinary navy blue store-bought cotton. Often this work is done on dark red cotton cloth with tiny, widely spaced white polka dots. Usually it's done by machine, but there was a period when it was embroidered by hand. Why is anyone's guess. Even doing it by machine would be a tremendous amount of work. Anyway, the pattern is completely geometric, mostly in gold with some red and two black lines.

The photographs here and in colorplate 32 show the designs from the black wool suit worn by the Chichicastenango men. As mentioned before, they do their own embroidery. The linear part is chain stitch and the flower petals are buttonhole in silk. The stitches are very small and very close together. The flower is on the side of the jacket, and you can see the way it embraces the pocket slit. The sunlike motif is on the flap that stands out on the side of the thigh. This motif seems to imply that from the sun come growth and plant life.

These people are highly tradition-minded, and they carry on their elaborate rituals, both

Chain stitch

Roman Catholic and animistic, with great concentration. The costume shown here is every bit a part of their tradition and is used only at ceremonies. Everyday attire is a simple white shirt and pants. The men are not traders and do not roam far afield, as do the men of many other Guatemalan villages. Perhaps their involvement with ritual, and the problems of daily life, keep them fully occupied.

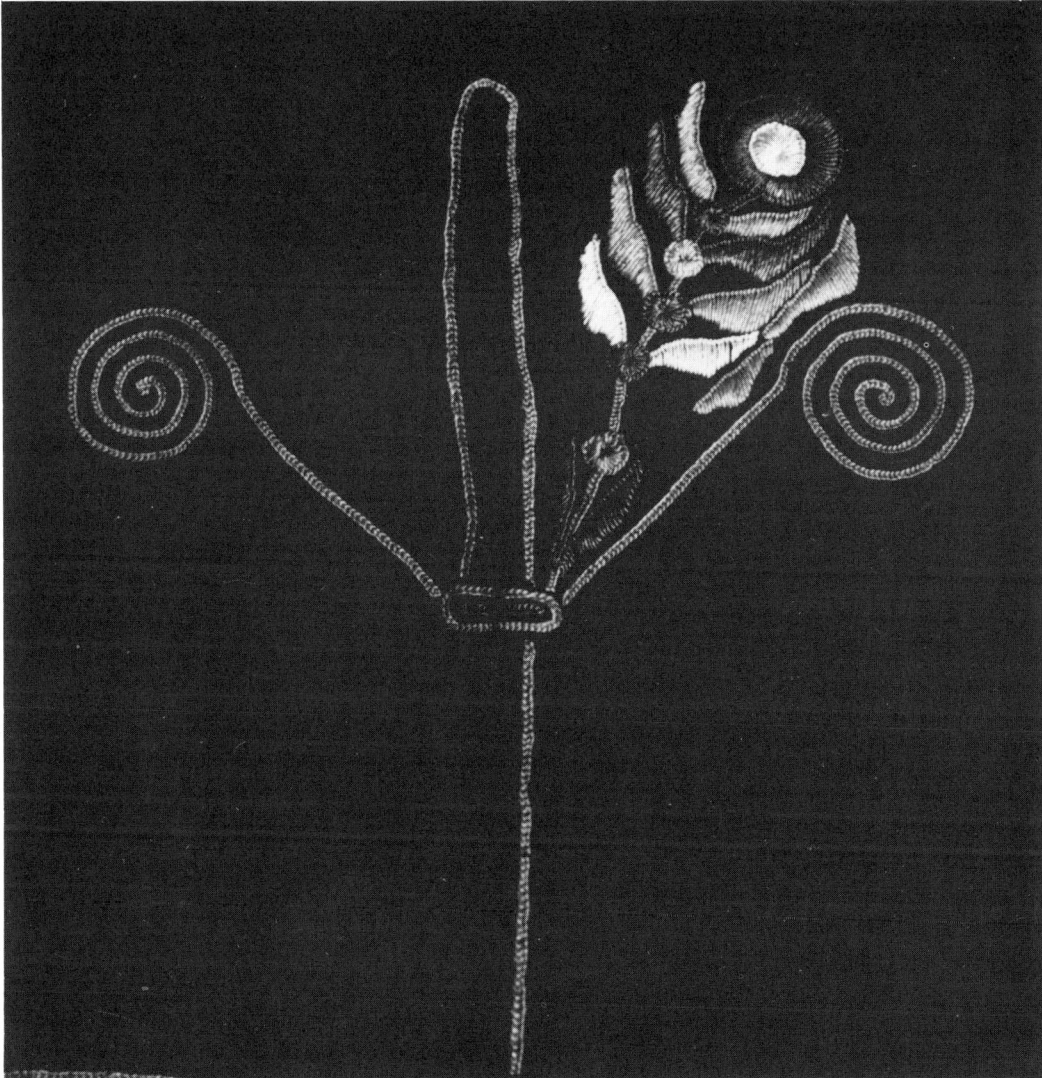

Motifs from a Chichicastenango man's suit. (Courtesy, Metropolitan Museum of
Art, New York; photograph: Charles Dorkins)

Needle Weaving

Needle weaving is another name for drawn work, which is done by removing threads, either warp or weft, in a given area and replacing them with threads interwoven by hand with a needle. Usually the remaining threads are fastened into bundles—sometimes all covered and sometimes left plain. The needle weaver must perforce finish the edges of the opening.

We have three examples.

Number one, in colorplate 33, is the edge for a Yucatecan *huipil*, or perhaps for the underskirt, called *fustan*, worn by older women. It seems as though traditionally the Mayans have done their embroidered edges in one color; this yellow one follows that tradition. Needle weaving may be a younger custom. It is called *xocbichuy*, meaning "to count" in Mayan. The Mayans have always excelled at counting. You can see the covered bundles of threads and the scalloped edges.

The example in colorplate 34 is from the front of the man's shirt worn in Zacatepec, Mexico. The material is white and hand-woven, and the design is done with regular embroidery floss in sections of pink, purple, orange, and green. In this instance the bundles of warp are all wrapped, and the edges are covered with double hemstitching.

The shoulder of a man's shirt from Ixtla-huaca, Mexico, has this work in "white on white." At the top and bottom are rows of double hemstitching. The rectangle of needle weaving is extremely complex. The warp threads are completely covered, and there is a great deal of reweaving, leaving spaces that form a diamond pattern. This is probably the most intricate work portrayed in this book. This type of needlework is fast dying out, and few examples are available. Quite possibly the technique came from the Spaniards.

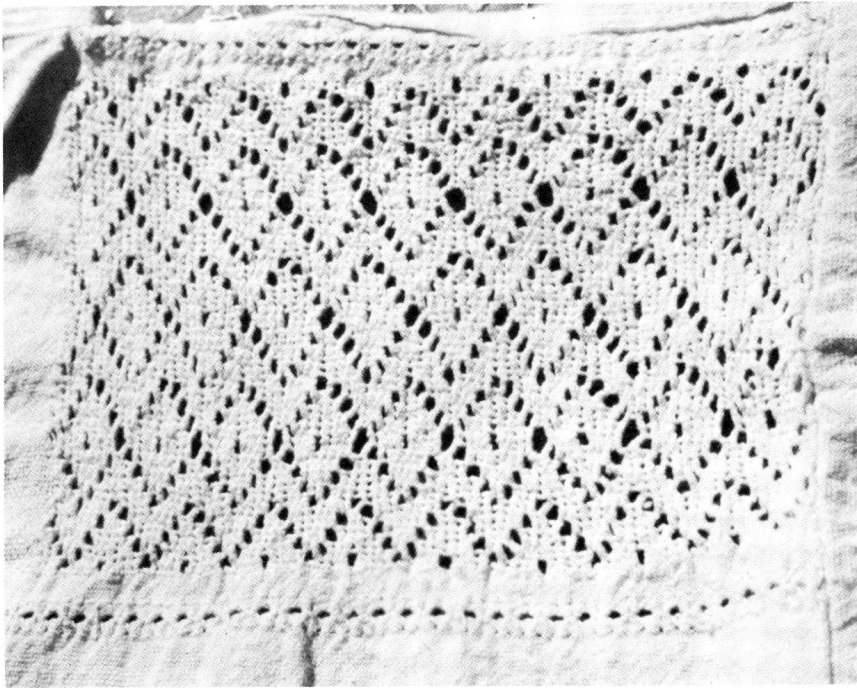

Intricate needle weaving
on a man's shirt from
Ixtlahuaca, Mexico. (Ruth
Erickson collection;
photograph:
Charles Dorkins)

✺ Index ✺